Eyewitness
SHIPWRECK

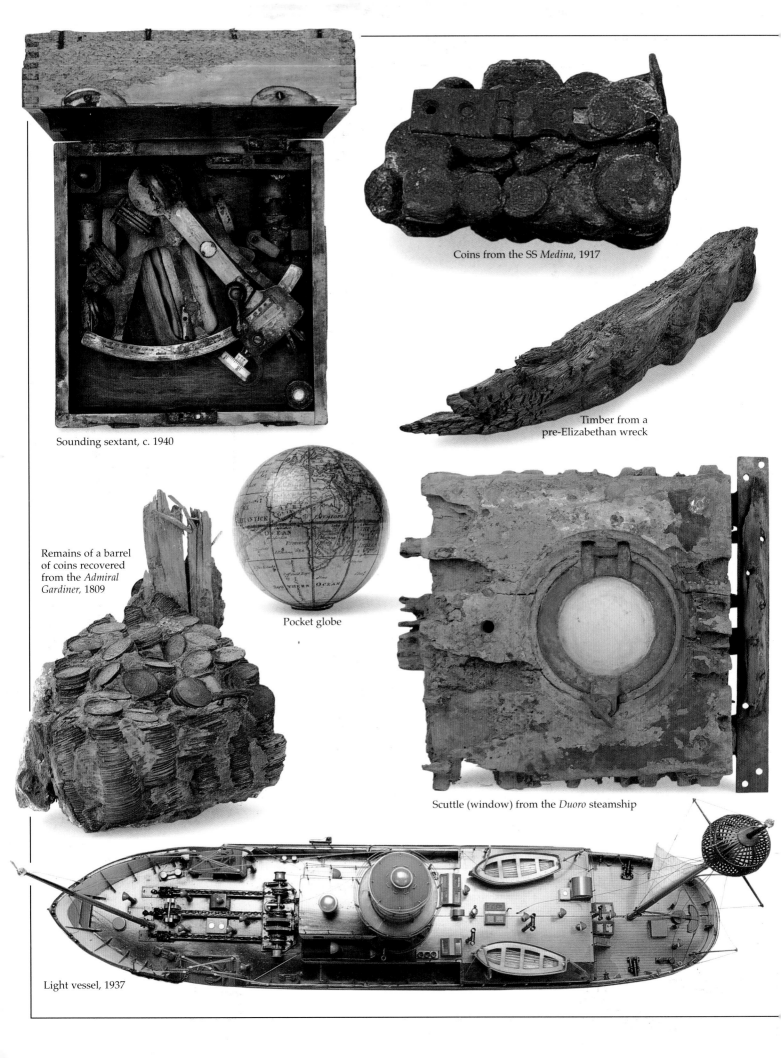

Sounding sextant, c. 1940

Coins from the SS *Medina*, 1917

Timber from a
pre-Elizabethan wreck

Remains of a barrel
of coins recovered
from the *Admiral
Gardiner*, 1809

Pocket globe

Scuttle (window) from the *Duoro* steamship

Light vessel, 1937

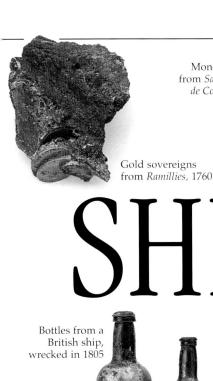

Money weights from *Santo Christo de Costello*, 1666

Mouth organs recovered from the sea after 100 years

Gold sovereigns from *Ramillies*, 1760

Eyewitness
SHIPWRECK

Written by
RICHARD PLATT

Photographed by
ALEX WILSON and
TINA CHAMBERS

Bottles from a British ship, wrecked in 1805

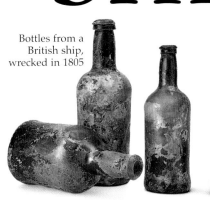

Lump of coins

Ornamental brass dolphins supported the binnacle (compass box) of the *Duoro* steamship

Hub of a World War I steamship found off the north coast of Cornwall, England

A Dorling Kindersley Book

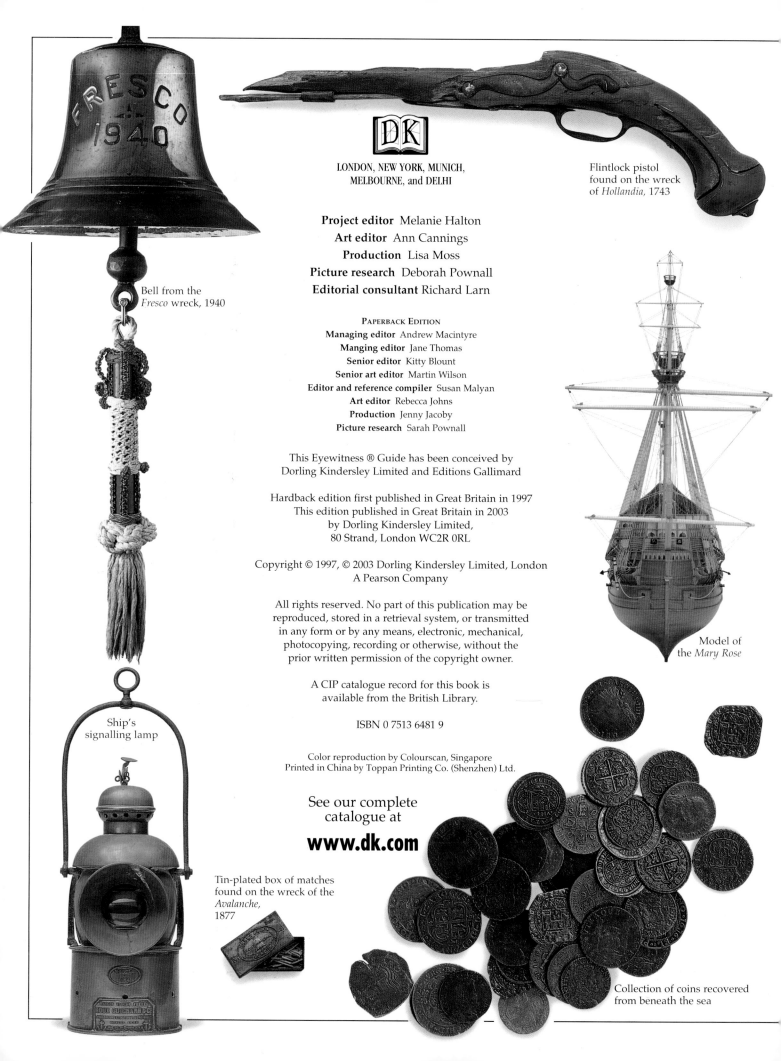

Bell from the
Fresco wreck, 1940

Flintlock pistol
found on the wreck
of *Hollandia,* 1743

DK

LONDON, NEW YORK, MUNICH,
MELBOURNE, and DELHI

Project editor Melanie Halton
Art editor Ann Cannings
Production Lisa Moss
Picture research Deborah Pownall
Editorial consultant Richard Larn

PAPERBACK EDITION
Managing editor Andrew Macintyre
Manging editor Jane Thomas
Senior editor Kitty Blount
Senior art editor Martin Wilson
Editor and reference compiler Susan Malyan
Art editor Rebecca Johns
Production Jenny Jacoby
Picture research Sarah Pownall

This Eyewitness ® Guide has been conceived by
Dorling Kindersley Limited and Editions Gallimard

Hardback edition first published in Great Britain in 1997
This edition published in Great Britain in 2003
by Dorling Kindersley Limited,
80 Strand, London WC2R 0RL

A CIP catalogue record for this book is
available from the British Library.

ISBN 0 7513 6481 9

Color reproduction by Colourscan, Singapore
Printed in China by Toppan Printing Co. (Shenzhen) Ltd.

See our complete
catalogue at

www.dk.com

Model of
the *Mary Rose*

Ship's
signalling lamp

Tin-plated box of matches
found on the wreck of the
Avalanche,
1877

Collection of coins recovered
from beneath the sea

Contents

Coral on a bottle

8
Rocks, wrecks, and rescues

10
Hazards of the sea

12
Ancient wrecks

14
First quests for wrecks

16
Far Eastern junks

18
Raising the Mary Rose

20
British shipwrecks

22
Wreck of the Armada

24
Lost in Lake Ontario

26
Unveiling the Vasa

28
"Unsinkable" Titanic

30
Oil tanker disasters

32
Navigation

34
Guiding lights

36
Communications

38
Shipwreck survivors

40
Air and sea rescues

42
Lifeboat equipment

44
Early diving

46
Scuba diving

48
Deep-sea exploration

50
Wreck location and recovery

52
Life on board ship

54
Lost cargoes

56
Reconstruction and preservation

58
The art of shipwrecks

60
Did you know?

62
Timeline

64
Find out more

66
Glossary

72
Index

Rocks, wrecks, and rescues

ASK ANYONE WHAT A SHIPWRECK IS, and they will probably say that it is the sinking of a vessel, or its destruction on a rocky coast. Some people may give a different reply: it is the remains of a ship resting on the seabed. Ask a sailor, and he will have yet another opinion: "Why, it's the end of the world for those on board!" Or perhaps you will hear salty yarns of thrilling escapes or daring rescues; of castaways, sunken treasure, and unsolved maritime mysteries. An archaeologist is likely to think that shipwrecks are fascinating views of the past, frozen in time like stopped clocks. All these answers are right: a shipwreck can be many things to many people. The pages that follow offer a glimpse of all these possibilities.

DRAMA AND TRAGEDY
Ancient Greek writers chose shipwrecks as subjects as long ago as the 8th century BC. Since then the drama of a shipwreck has continued to fascinate writers and painters (pp. 58–59). Artist Samuel Owen painted this scene in 1837.

TREASURES FROM THE DEEP
Not all shipwrecks contain gold and silver in rotting chests! But treasure wrecks do exist, and the possibility of discovering a fortune lures countless divers to explore the seabed.

Forty boxes of Mexican liberty dollars were found on the Crescent City *steamship, wrecked in 1871*

SAVING LIVES AT SEA
When ships are wrecked near the shore, a lifeboat (pp. 40–43) speeds to the area of the disaster. The lifeboat crew plucks survivors from the ocean, or rescues them from the vessel if it is still afloat. A stretcher like this one is used to rescue casualties without making their injuries worse.

Belts hold the casualty securely in place

Handles help lifeboat crew to fix stretcher to rescue line

Rigid frame protects against bumps

Flaps stop casualty's body from moving

ITALIAN TRAGEDY
Navigation equipment (pp. 32–33) reduces the risk of shipwreck, but it cannot eliminate the danger altogether. The *Stockholm*, which rammed the *Andrea Doria* (above) one foggy night in 1956 appeared as an approaching blip on the radar screen, but the Italian passenger liner could not turn quickly enough to avoid collision.

AIR-SEA RESCUE
When a ship is in distress in the open ocean, aircraft can quickly scan vast areas. If they locate a liferaft or floating wreckage, rescue helicopters (pp. 41, 43) take over, winching victims to safety. Air and sea rescue services cooperate closely.

STORMY WATERS
Gales wrecked countless ships in the days before steam power. A sailing ship driven on to a lee shore (a coastline facing the wind) had almost no way to escape being wrecked.

STEERING TO DISASTER
The sea can prevent human exploration of a wreck for many centuries, but it does not protect it from marine life. Sea creatures can make a meal of woodwork, and reduced this ship's steering wheel to hub and spokes in just 90 years.

Wheel spokes eaten away by marine life

GHOST SHIP
Not every shipping disaster leads to a wreck: some end much more mysteriously. Cast adrift on the Atlantic Ocean, the sailing ship *Mary Celeste* was found empty but undamaged in December 1872. An abandoned meal lay on a table in the cabin, and the cargo of alcohol was untouched. Nobody has ever been able to explain what happened to the crew.

DIVING FOR PICTURES
The invention of scuba (pp. 46–47) in the 1940s made it very much easier for archaeologists to study wrecks. This commercial diver is equipped to video his find with a head-mounted camera.

9

Hazards of the sea

THE SEAFARER'S LIFE is a dangerous one. Rocks may punch holes in a ship's hull; ice may crush it. Wind and surf can break up a ship, or fire can burn it to its water-line. These and many other hazards still destroy vessels large and small, even those that have strong steel hulls and powerful engines to help them steer clear of danger. If shipwreck comes, ocean waters quickly drown those unlucky sailors who are unable to reach a lifeboat. Swimming is a surprisingly modern skill, and many mariners of the past lacked it. When the British naval ship *Lichfield* was wrecked in 1758, only 60 sailors out of a crew of 350 could swim. Often nobody on board could swim. One crew, whose vessel ran aground, tied a rescue rope to the ship's pig and let it swim them to safety. No wonder, then, that only half of all sailors died of old age. The sea, and countless other maritime hazards, consumed the rest.

WAVES
High winds whip up ocean waves of terrifying size. Waves are most likely to damage a ship at sea by swamping it with water, rather than tipping it over. The pressure and suction of waves crashing against the shore breaks up any ship that runs aground.

BLOWING IN THE WIND
Buoys – floating markers – indicate the position of many known hazards to ships. A chain or cable anchors the buoy to the seabed, and its distinctive shape and colour identify the hazard it marks. European nations introduced the first wooden buoys in the late 15th and early 16th centuries.

FOG
Sea fog forms when warm air blows across cold ocean water. Before the invention of radar, thick fog made navigation extremely hazardous: helmsmen steering the boat relied on the sound of foghorns and ships' bells to avoid grounding or collisions.

SANDBANKS
In shallow water, banks of sand can easily trap a ship as the tide goes out. Currents move sandbanks, so a ship's charts can only indicate roughly where they lie.

CORAL REEFS
In tropical regions, a coral reef – built from the chalky skeletons of marine creatures – surrounds many islands. The biggest ships anchor in deep water beyond the reef, but smaller vessels try to find a safe channel through the sharp barrier. Not all succeed.

WRECK BUOY
In narrow straits and shallow stretches of water, wrecked ships can themselves obstruct the channel, thereby increasing the likelihood of another wreck occurring. In the English Channel, one of the busiest shipping lanes in the world, there are the remains of more than 2,000 shipwrecks. Buoys mark the positions of the most dangerous ones.

WARNING
DANGER
UNEXPLODED
AMMUNITION
KEEP AT LEAST
700 FEET
FROM WRECK
WRECK

Around the North and South Pole the ocean is permanently frozen. During the winter the area covered by ice grows, as more sea water freezes to form pack ice (large masses of floating ice). Ships, such as the *Pandora* (right), which was caught in the ice in 1876, are stranded there until the spring thaw. Drifting pack ice can create tremendous pressure: enough to crush and sink a wooden-hulled ship.

Wind disc for tracking the path of the typhoon

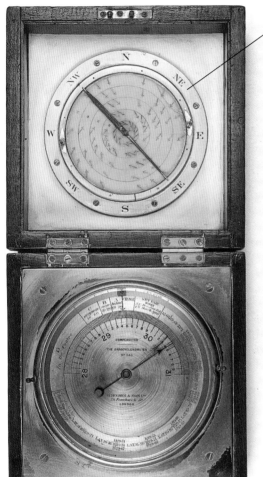

Flashing navigational light

Radio antenna

Propeller wind vane calculates wind speed and direction

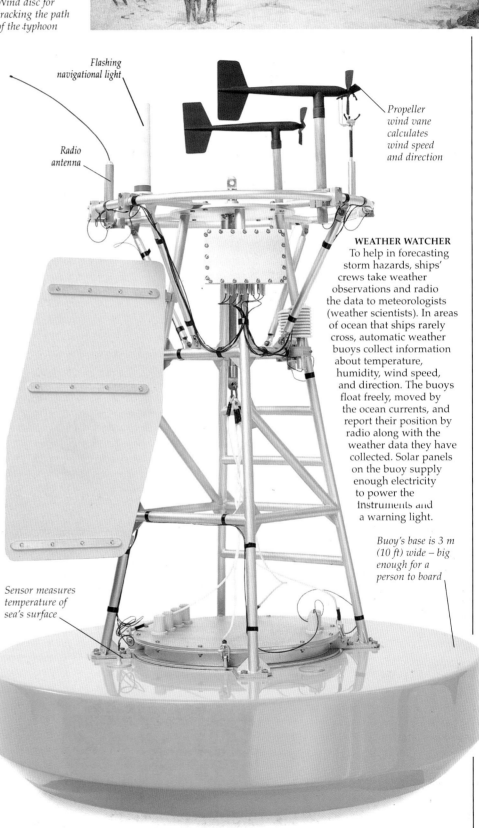

WEATHER WATCHER

To help in forecasting storm hazards, ships' crews take weather observations and radio the data to meteorologists (weather scientists). In areas of ocean that ships rarely cross, automatic weather buoys collect information about temperature, humidity, wind speed, and direction. The buoys float freely, moved by the ocean currents, and report their position by radio along with the weather data they have collected. Solar panels on the buoy supply enough electricity to power the instruments and a warning light.

Buoy's base is 3 m (10 ft) wide – big enough for a person to board

Sensor measures temperature of sea's surface

AVOIDING THE STORM

Since 1960, orbiting satellites have enabled hurricanes to be tracked and warnings to be sent to ships. But weather forecasts were not always so dependable. In the past, mariners relied on instruments such as this "baryocyclometer". Its lower dial is a barometer that shows the pressure of the air. The upper dial suggests the safest course to steer, based on the wind direction.

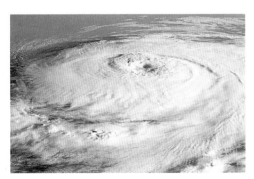

HURRICANE

Cyclone, typhoon, and hurricane all mean the same thing: a gigantic revolving tropical storm. Hurricanes bring torrential rains, winds as fast as 240 km/h (150 mph), and mountainous seas. Some are powerful enough to pick up yachts and throw them on to land.

Ancient wrecks

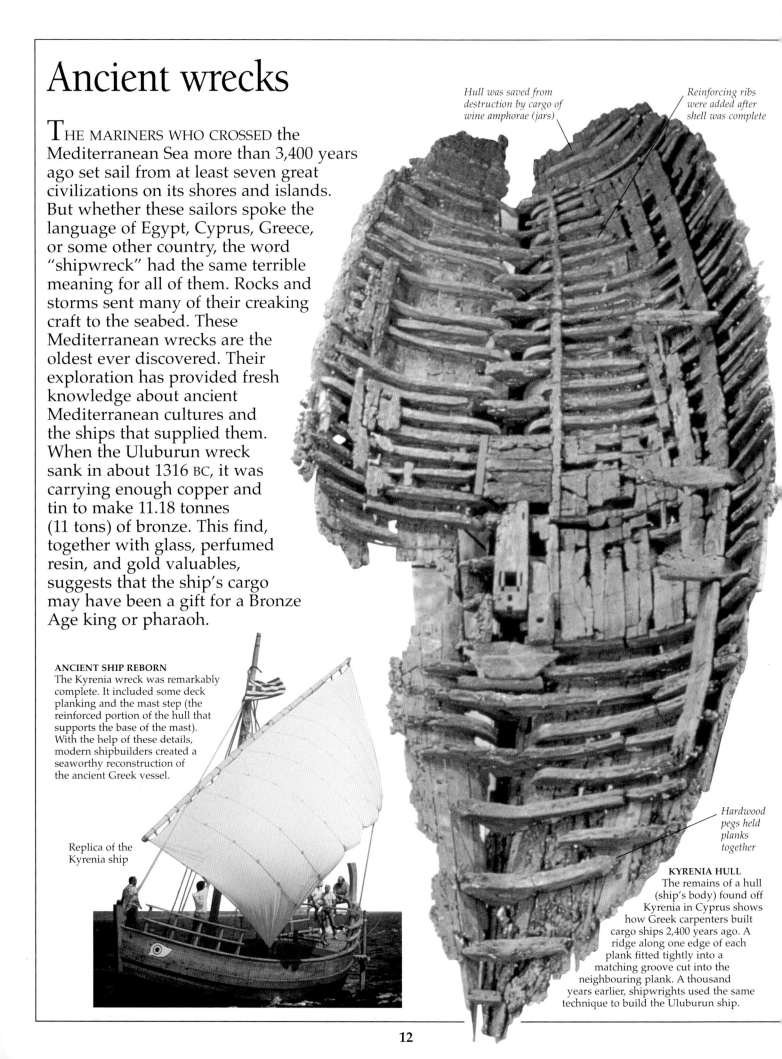

THE MARINERS WHO CROSSED the Mediterranean Sea more than 3,400 years ago set sail from at least seven great civilizations on its shores and islands. But whether these sailors spoke the language of Egypt, Cyprus, Greece, or some other country, the word "shipwreck" had the same terrible meaning for all of them. Rocks and storms sent many of their creaking craft to the seabed. These Mediterranean wrecks are the oldest ever discovered. Their exploration has provided fresh knowledge about ancient Mediterranean cultures and the ships that supplied them. When the Uluburun wreck sank in about 1316 BC, it was carrying enough copper and tin to make 11.18 tonnes (11 tons) of bronze. This find, together with glass, perfumed resin, and gold valuables, suggests that the ship's cargo may have been a gift for a Bronze Age king or pharaoh.

Hull was saved from destruction by cargo of wine amphorae (jars)

Reinforcing ribs were added after shell was complete

Hardwood pegs held planks together

ANCIENT SHIP REBORN
The Kyrenia wreck was remarkably complete. It included some deck planking and the mast step (the reinforced portion of the hull that supports the base of the mast). With the help of these details, modern shipbuilders created a seaworthy reconstruction of the ancient Greek vessel.

Replica of the Kyrenia ship

KYRENIA HULL
The remains of a hull (ship's body) found off Kyrenia in Cyprus shows how Greek carpenters built cargo ships 2,400 years ago. A ridge along one edge of each plank fitted tightly into a matching groove cut into the neighbouring plank. A thousand years earlier, shipwrights used the same technique to build the Uluburun ship.

ULUBURUN

In 1984, a Turkish diver searching for sponges found the world's oldest shipwreck known of at that time. The metal ingots raised were the first of hundreds that archaeologists later recovered. Trinkets and amphorae (left) littered the wreck, which has been named after its location – Uluburun.

Unknown goddess holds a gazelle in each hand

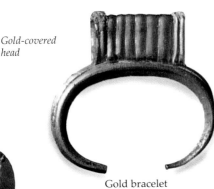

Gold-covered head

Gold bracelet

Medallion with Canaanite star design

CANAANITE JEWELLERY

The discovery on the Uluburun wreck of trinkets and raw materials from Canaan (now part of Israel) gave historians a clearer view of ancient Mediterranean trade. They used to believe that merchants from Mycenae (an ancient Greek city-state) controlled shipping. Jewellery (above and left), ingots, and glass from the wreck show that the Canaanites rivalled them.

PROTECTIVE GODDESS

A bronze statuette from the Uluburun wreck shows a naked goddess. Her pose is typical of a blessing goddess, and suggests that she was a sacred charm who protected the ship. American archaeologist George Bass, who led the team raising the wreck, believes she indicates that the ship sailed from Syria.

Bronze statuette

Ivory hinges

THE WORLD'S OLDEST BOOK

Ivory hinges held together the carved wooden panels of this writing board. Divers found it in a jar of pomegranates on the Uluburun ship. Its owner scratched out messages in the beeswax that covered the recessed inner surfaces. If the words had survived, it would be the world's oldest book.

First quests for wrecks

A SHIPWRECK IS A TRAGEDY for the families of those who drown. But it is also an expensive calamity for the owner, or the merchant with goods in the hold. Recovering these enormous financial losses was the aim of the first desperate attempts to raise ships, or their cargoes. Shipwrecks in shallow water were easy to salvage. Swimmers who could hold their breath for a minute or more plundered the wreck before surfacing for air. Wrecks in deep water, however, were out of reach and most rotted on the seabed until the invention of diving suits, around 1830. Scientific study of wrecks under water started a century later, but archaeologists only began to supervise divers and to record wrecks methodically in the 1950s.

FIRST DIVERS
With practice, divers holding their breath could reach depths as great as 50 m (165 ft). Often they returned from the seabed clutching not the pearls or sponges that they were seeking, but treasure from a forgotten shipwreck.

VASA SALVAGE
Building the *Vasa* (pp. 26–27) warship had cost a twentieth of all Sweden's wealth, so her sinking in 1628 was a huge loss. Divers working inside bells reached the wreck soon after the disaster and recovered many of the ship's valuable guns.

RAISING THE ROYAL GEORGE
Wrecks of warships held a fortune in cannons. One cannon could pay the wages of 20 sailors for a year. In 1782, the *Royal George* sank with 100 guns. There were several attempts to raise the ship and its cannons, but all failed. The wreck was blown up with explosives in 1848 to clear the English harbour that it blocked.

COLOURFUL CANNONS
When the *Mary Rose* (pp. 18–19) sank in 1545, salvage divers travelled from Venice to try to rescue the wreck, but they only managed to find a few guns. Nearly three centuries later, John and Charles Deane raised these cannons, using a pioneering diving suit of their own design.

SUNKEN SPANISH SILVER
In 1702 an Anglo-Dutch attack at Vigo Bay (right), on Spain's Atlantic coast, sank a hoard of silver that has lured treasure-seekers ever since. The silver was on board ships returning from Spanish colonies in the Americas. The first expedition to find the lost bullion began in 1720. It was failure, just like the 30 that followed.

PHILOSOPHER'S GLASSY STARE
Among the treasures that the Greek navy recovered from the Antikythera wreck (below) was this spectacular bust of a philosopher, complete with glass eyes. Unfortunately, the divers who found the wreck sold many smaller bronze statues before reporting it.

POSEIDON STATUE
When the net of a fishing boat fouled (caught) on the bed of the Aegean Sea off Cape Artemisium in 1928, divers went down to investigate. They found a spectacular life-size bronze statue of Poseidon, Greek god of the sea. The wreck has since been lost again.

Mainsail is decorated with mythological beasts

ANTIKYTHERA WRECK
A sponge diver working off the Greek island of Antikythera in 1900 surfaced raving about rotting corpses. What he had seen were statues in the wreck of a Roman cargo ship, much like this model. A government search revealed art treasures – and a mysterious box of gears that may have been used to predict the moon's phases.

Mainbrace supports the mainmast

Far Eastern junks

FOR FOUR CENTURIES the largest, safest ships in the world carried vast cargoes of porcelain. These great vessels were not Spanish galleons or Dutch East Indiamen; they were Chinese junks. China has an ancient tradition of boat building, and by the 15th century Chinese shipwrights were making big ocean-going vessels. When they invented stern-post rudders (p. 17), Arab mariners copied the design and took it to the West. Watertight compartments stopped junks from sinking 700 years before European ships incorporated this crucial safety feature. By 1450, junks were as big and seaworthy as 19th-century European ships. Even these sophisticated Chinese vessels, however, could not avoid the sea's power, and many of their porcelain cargoes ended up on the seabed.

TRADING JUNK
The junk was an ideal vessel for trading on the coast and in China's great rivers. Its flat-bottomed hull and lifting rudder made it easy to beach, and allowed the junk to sail in shallow water.

POISON TESTER
Much of the Sinan wreck cargo was green-glazed earthenware that Europeans called celadon. The superstitious believed the pottery changed colour or broke if the food it contained was poisoned.

CARGO FROM THE SINAN WRECK
Venetian explorer Marco Polo (1254–1324) might have eaten from crockery very similar to this when he visited the court of China's ruler Kublai Khan. This cargo of porcelain was on its way from China to Japan when the Sinan ship carrying it was wrecked off Korea's coast around 1323.

MAN–WOMAN GOD
A small pottery statuette raised almost intact from the Sinan wreck represents the Buddhist god, Kuan-yin. This popular god was neither male nor female, so the figurine has a flowing female figure – and a bushy moustache!

FIGURES FROM THE DEEP
A fisherman's catch of porcelain off Vietnam's south coast led the state salvage company to a junk wrecked 300 years previously. Named after the nearby port of Vung Tau, the junk had been burned to its water-line before sinking. These white porcelain figures were part of its rich cargo.

STERN-POST RUDDERS
The stern-post rudder on this Keying junk made steering easy and safe because the rudder was in line with the ship's keel. European sailors used an oar hung over the ship's starboard side until they adopted this Chinese idea around 1200.

VUNG TAU VASES
Vietnamese divers recovered an astonishing quantity of porcelain from the Vung Tau wreck. Experts believe that the pots were among the first made in China, specially for export to the West. Many of the shapes and patterns show signs of European influences – some vases are even patterned with houses similar to Dutch buildings of the time.

CHINESE PIRATE JUNKS
Not all junks traded peacefully. Chinese pirates armed their junks with small swivel guns and larger carriage guns that fired a ball as big as an orange. Seven-hundred-strong fleets of these pirate junks terrorized the South China Seas. Western nations policing the seas could not compete with them until they introduced steam-driven paddleships. This illustration shows the British East India Company's steamship *Nemesis* destroying pirate junks at Anson's Bay in 1841.

TOWERING TEA BOWLS
The Vung Tau cargo sank around 1690, at a time when Chinese porcelain was fashionable and expensive in Europe. Within a century, however, European potters had discovered how to make thin, ceramic bowls like these for themselves. Inferior Chinese imports had also swamped the market, and ships brought porcelain from China only as ballast – to aid stability.

Raising the Mary Rose

ONE SUMMER'S DAY IN 1545, England's king Henry VIII (1491–1547) stood watching his navy in the Solent, a sheltered channel on the south coast of Britain. The fleet, which included the second-largest ship in the navy – the *Mary Rose* – was sailing to fight invading French ships. It should have been a simple, well-rehearsed routine, but on this day, it was not. A breeze probably filled the sails before they were in place and the *Mary Rose* heeled (tilted). When the lowest row of gunports dipped below the water, the ship was doomed. The sea rushed in, sinking the *Mary Rose* and drowning more than 650 sailors and soldiers, including the officer in command, Sir George Carew. Within minutes, only the ship's mast tops were visible above the water.

PORTRAIT OF A QUEEN
The *Mary Rose* was named after the king's favourite sister Mary Tudor, and the royal flower emblem. The only surviving picture of the ship was painted the year after she sank. It shows a powerful, majestic, purpose-built warship.

ROYAL CANNONS
Henry VIII ordered shipwrights to build the *Mary Rose* in the first year of his reign as part of his effort to increase England's military might. To equip his enlarged navy with the brass and iron cannons it needed, Henry appointed a royal gun founder (caster). Henry's gun foundries used so much brass that in 1510 there was a world shortage of tin, which was mixed with copper to make brass.

Starboard side
of the *Mary Rose*

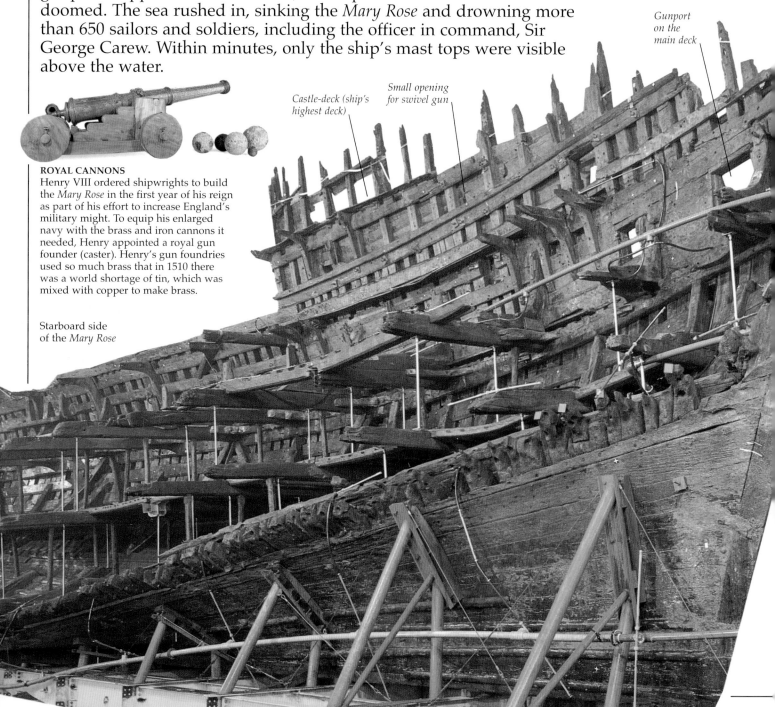

*Gunport
on the
main deck*

*Castle-deck (ship's
highest deck)*

*Small opening
for swivel gun*

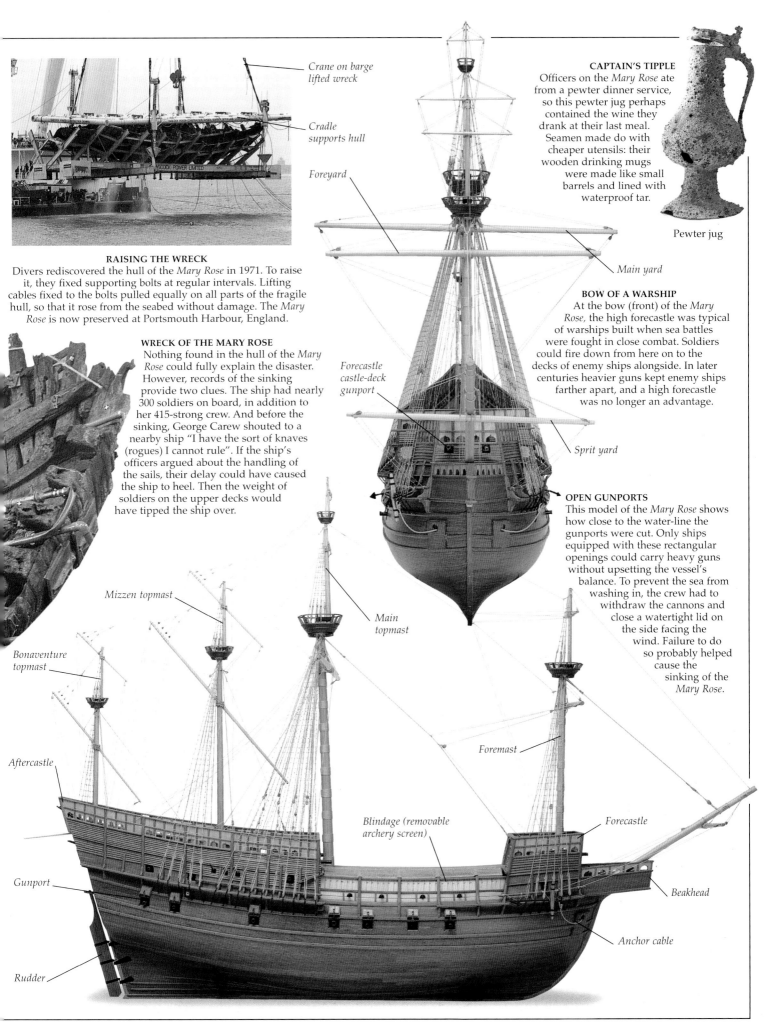

Crane on barge lifted wreck

Cradle supports hull

Foreyard

CAPTAIN'S TIPPLE
Officers on the *Mary Rose* ate from a pewter dinner service, so this pewter jug perhaps contained the wine they drank at their last meal. Seamen made do with cheaper utensils: their wooden drinking mugs were made like small barrels and lined with waterproof tar.

Pewter jug

RAISING THE WRECK
Divers rediscovered the hull of the *Mary Rose* in 1971. To raise it, they fixed supporting bolts at regular intervals. Lifting cables fixed to the bolts pulled equally on all parts of the fragile hull, so that it rose from the seabed without damage. The *Mary Rose* is now preserved at Portsmouth Harbour, England.

WRECK OF THE MARY ROSE
Nothing found in the hull of the *Mary Rose* could fully explain the disaster. However, records of the sinking provide two clues. The ship had nearly 300 soldiers on board, in addition to her 415-strong crew. And before the sinking, George Carew shouted to a nearby ship "I have the sort of knaves (rogues) I cannot rule". If the ship's officers argued about the handling of the sails, their delay could have caused the ship to heel. Then the weight of soldiers on the upper decks would have tipped the ship over.

Main yard

BOW OF A WARSHIP
At the bow (front) of the *Mary Rose*, the high forecastle was typical of warships built when sea battles were fought in close combat. Soldiers could fire down from here on to the decks of enemy ships alongside. In later centuries heavier guns kept enemy ships farther apart, and a high forecastle was no longer an advantage.

Forecastle castle-deck gunport

Sprit yard

OPEN GUNPORTS
This model of the *Mary Rose* shows how close to the water-line the gunports were cut. Only ships equipped with these rectangular openings could carry heavy guns without upsetting the vessel's balance. To prevent the sea from washing in, the crew had to withdraw the cannons and close a watertight lid on the side facing the wind. Failure to do so probably helped cause the sinking of the *Mary Rose*.

Mizzen topmast

Bonaventure topmast

Main topmast

Aftercastle

Foremast

Gunport

Blindage (removable archery screen)

Forecastle

Beakhead

Anchor cable

Rudder

British shipwrecks

BRITAIN'S LINKS WITH THE SEA are ancient – nowhere in Britain is farther than 118 km (73 miles) from the sea. Britain's coastal waters are treacherous, however, even for mariners who know them well. Jagged rocks and sucking sandbanks guard the shoreline. Some of the highest tides in the world wash the country's ports. Learning to escape these hazards made British sailors among the world's best, and by the 18th century Great Britain was a powerful maritime nation. A popular song, written in 1740, even claimed that "Britannia rules the waves". But no nation, however great, can ever really control the awesome power of the oceans, and British mariners knew they risked shipwreck on every trip.

SAILOR'S BEST FRIEND
There is no reason to believe that drunkeness caused the wreck of the *Ramillies*, but all ships of the time carried plenty of drink. Officers often drank three bottles (2.3 litres or half a gallon) of wine a day. Ordinary seamen's fondness for grog (rum and water) earned it the nickname "the sailor's best friend".

Ramillies

The *Ramillies* was a first-rate man-of-war: one of the largest in the British navy. But when she made her last, ill-fated trip she was 96 years old and leaked badly. In February 1760, the *Ramillies* left the port of Plymouth in south-west England. On her return she became trapped in Bigbury Bay, some 20 km (12 miles) to the east. There, hurricane-force winds drove the ship on to the rocks, killing 700 people.

Plate and spoons

Leather shoes

Buckles

WRECK REMAINS
Wreckage from the *Ramillies* filled Bigbury Bay, and local people sneaked off with anything that they could carry. Salvage work recovered some of the guns, but the wreck then lay undisturbed until 1906. Divers have since recovered hundreds of artefacts, and a display of them at the Charlestown Shipwreck Centre in St. Austell, Cornwall creates a vivid picture of life on board the doomed warship.

ON THE ROCKS
Wind and waves snapped the masts of the *Ramillies* like matches, and flung the crew on to the rocks. The terrifying experience drove one officer completely mad; he stayed with the sinking ship and sang as it went down.

Royal Charter

The wrecking of the iron-hulled passenger and cargo ship *Royal Charter* (left) occurred in October, 1859. The ship had just made a record run from Australia to Britain, but she could not compete with strong winds off the Welsh Isle of Anglesey which caused the ship to drift on to the rocks. One seaman swam ashore with a rescue line, but a huge wave broke off the stern of the ship where most of the passengers were sheltering. Some of the 459 people who died in the wreck drowned because they jumped overboard wearing money belts full of gold.

Candleholder

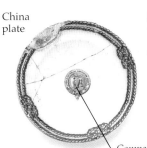

China plate

Silver-plated teapot

Lid is stuck to handle

Company crest

Vase

Gold sovereigns

Duoro

Coffee, diamonds, and gold filled the hold of the mail ship *Duoro* as she steamed from South America to Britain in 1882. On 1st April, just two days away from her destination, a collision with a Spanish vessel holed the *Duoro*. Most of the passengers and crew escaped in the lifeboats, but her precious cargo sank 450 m (1,500 ft) to the bottom of the Bay of Biscay, off Spain's coast.

China cup

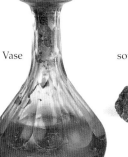

Duoro's compass support

"LOOK OUT!"
The *Duoro's* small scuttles, or windows (above), did little to ventilate her cabins, and a passenger who went on deck in search of fresh air spotted the nearing Spanish ship. The crew ignored his warnings, with tragic results.

China plate

FINDING THE WRECK OF THE DUORO
A salvage team knew they had located the *Duoro* wreck in 1995 when they recovered a porcelain plate. Its sea horse crest identified it as coming from a Royal Mail ship. The salvors raised 28,000 gold sovereigns from the bullion room.

Wreck of the Armada

SPANISH PEOPLE FELT SURE OF VICTORY when their navy set off to invade England in May 1588. They called the 130 warships the *Armada Invincible* – the unbeatable war fleet. When they reached England, however, the Armada's weapons could not match the cannons of the English fleet, and drifting fire ships (vessels deliberately set ablaze) forced them to scatter. Gales blew the Spaniards north and prevented them from picking up reinforcements. The Armada had to return to Spain by sailing round Ireland, where storms wrecked nearly 30 ships on the Atlantic coast. Four centuries later, archaeologists have excavated five of the wrecks. From gold trinkets – and ordinary items such as rigging – they are learning more about the ill-fated Armada and the lives of the 11,000 Spanish sailors who perished around British shores.

SPAIN'S RULER
Philip II, king of Spain from 1556 to 1598, ruled a vast empire, including the Netherlands. A revolt there threatened Spanish rule, so Philip launched the Armada hoping to end English support for Dutch rebels, and to stamp out English piracy against Spanish ships.

Course the Armada ships were trying to steer

Gold and silver coins found on an Armada wreck

BREAKING THE RULES
The Spanish ships expected to fight by the traditional method of boarding English vessels to capture or destroy them. The English ships, however, had more cannons and defeated the Spaniards by firing from afar, avoiding close combat.

USELESS INSTRUMENT
The *Girona's* navigator would have used this astrolabe to check the ship's route by measuring the Sun's position. But the Armada sailed home in fog and cloud, which hid the Sun, and navigation errors led many ships to founder on the rocks.

ARMADA ROUTE
The Spanish fleet was first spotted on the 30th July, 1588 as it sailed into the English Channel, and was followed closely by English warships. On the 8th August, 1588 the decisive Battle of Gravelines broke out. Although defeated, the Spanish lost only two ships. Most of the losses came later, caused not by English victories, but by shipwrecks.

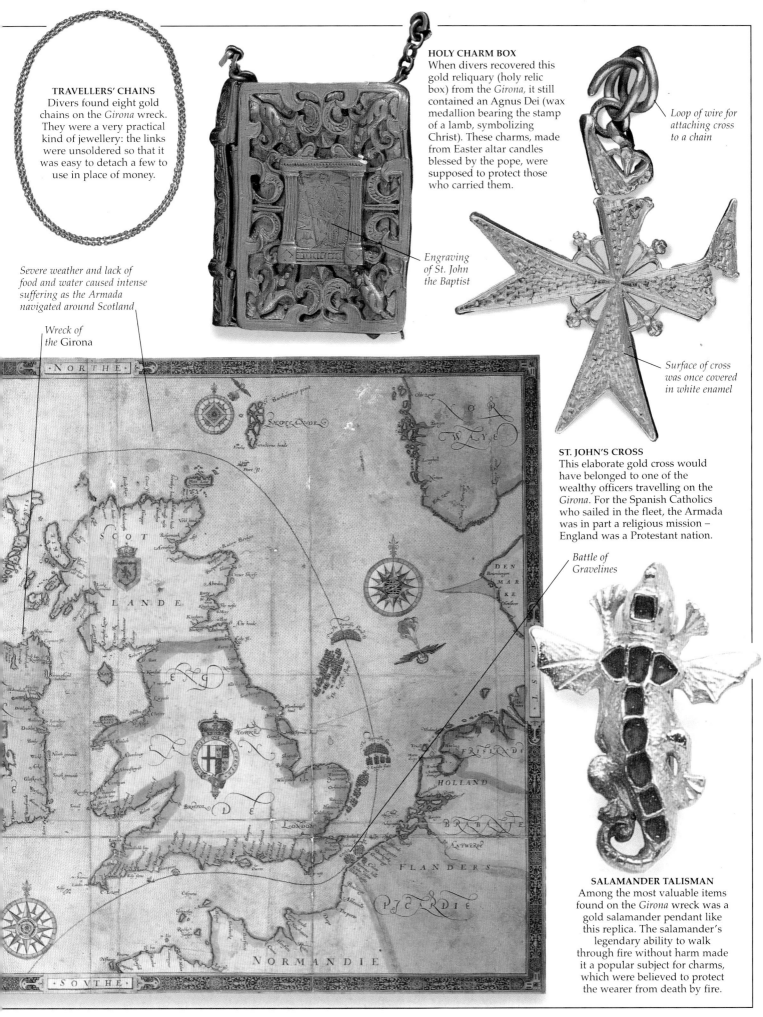

TRAVELLERS' CHAINS
Divers found eight gold chains on the *Girona* wreck. They were a very practical kind of jewellery: the links were unsoldered so that it was easy to detach a few to use in place of money.

HOLY CHARM BOX
When divers recovered this gold reliquary (holy relic box) from the *Girona,* it still contained an Agnus Dei (wax medallion bearing the stamp of a lamb, symbolizing Christ). These charms, made from Easter altar candles blessed by the pope, were supposed to protect those who carried them.

Loop of wire for attaching cross to a chain

Engraving of St. John the Baptist

Surface of cross was once covered in white enamel

ST. JOHN'S CROSS
This elaborate gold cross would have belonged to one of the wealthy officers travelling on the *Girona*. For the Spanish Catholics who sailed in the fleet, the Armada was in part a religious mission – England was a Protestant nation.

Severe weather and lack of food and water caused intense suffering as the Armada navigated around Scotland

Wreck of the Girona

Battle of Gravelines

SALAMANDER TALISMAN
Among the most valuable items found on the *Girona* wreck was a gold salamander pendant like this replica. The salamander's legendary ability to walk through fire without harm made it a popular subject for charms, which were believed to protect the wearer from death by fire.

Lost in Lake Ontario

IN TERMS OF POWER, the United States Navy was a minnow to Britain's shark when the two countries went to war in 1812. The British navy had 800 warships; the Americans had only 16. The United States hurriedly built ships, but also converted merchant vessels, including Great Lakes schooners the *Hamilton*, and the *Scourge*. Both of these schooners were more used to carrying coal than cannons, and made poor warships. The weight of a cargo low in the hold helps to make a ship steadier; heavy cannons on the deck have the opposite effect. "It'll be our coffin," cursed the crew of the *Scourge*, and a squall in 1813 proved them right. The wind turned both the *Scourge* and the *Hamilton* over in an instant and they quickly sank, killing all but eight of the crew from the two ships. The icy waters of Lake Ontario hid the ships until 1975, when a remote-controlled camera recorded these remarkable images of the lost schooners.

THE WAR OF 1812
The United States fought Great Britain from 1812–1815 because of British interference with American trade with Napoleonic France. They also wanted to put a stop to the British navy's practice of removing British sailors from American ships and forcing them back into naval service.

Hamilton figurehead

LADY HAMILTON
Until she joined the navy, the *Hamilton* was called the *Diana*, and her figurehead shows a graceful 19th-century American lady. The fresh, cold water of Lake Ontario preserved much of the intricate detail of the carving.

SHADOWY SHIP
Side-scan sonar (p. 50) provided this ghostly image of the *Hamilton* wreck. The ship stands upright on the bed of the lake, with its hull fully intact. The sonar "shadow" clearly shows the schooner's two masts, and outlines on the deck pick out the positions of hatches, cannons, boats, and other equipment. A research vessel from the Canada Centre for Inland Waters made the image after locating the ship in 88 m (290 ft) of water.

SUBMERGED SCOURGE
A remotely operated underwater vehicle (ROV) photographed and video-taped the wrecks. This artist's reconstruction, drawn from the pictures and video footage, shows the ROV at work above the *Scourge*. Many of the details it recorded feature in a dramatic account of the sinking written by Ned Myers, one of the eight survivors. He described it to American novelist James Fenimore Cooper in 1843. Cooper made the *Scourge* wreck a highlight of his biography *Ned Myers; or A Life Before the Mast*.

Nelson leads the Scourge into battle

FIGUREHEAD FOR THE FOE
The *Scourge* had been a Canadian merchant vessel called *Lord Nelson* before she was captured by the Americans and converted to a warship. The figurehead of the British naval hero, Admiral Horatio Nelson, led the *Scourge* into attacks on British ships! Although this sculpture has two arms, Nelson actually lost an arm during battle 15 years before this ship was built.

Figurehead of the
Scourge warship

HAMILTON SMASHERS
Nicknamed "the Smasher" by British crews who faced it, the carronade was a short gun that could do terrible damage when ships fought at close range. The *Hamilton* carried eight carronades; the 8-kg (18-lb) iron balls which each gun fired were roughly three-quarters the size of a bowling ball. The ROV's camera picked out this carronade's barrel resting on its mounting aboard the *Scourge*.

Unveiling the Vasa

MARINERS KNOW that their voyage is always in danger of ending suddenly if they are shipwrecked, but for the crew of the *Vasa* the end came almost as soon as their vessel was launched. This magnificent sailing ship was to be the pride of the Swedish navy. On 10th August, 1628, the *Vasa* set out across Stockholm harbour on her maiden voyage. Shortly after the crew had raised the sails, having travelled just 1,300 m (4,625 ft), a gust of wind blew the ship over. Within minutes the *Vasa* sank in 33 m (110 ft) of water. Three centuries later, archaeologists turned this tragedy into triumph. The wreck they raised in 1961 is the most complete example of a 17th-century naval vessel ever to have been discovered.

TOP-HEAVY WARSHIP
The *Vasa* had far too much weight above the water-line. She could stay upright in the sheltered harbour, but the slightest breeze was enough to capsize the top-heavy gunship.

SAILOR'S LAST MEAL
The wreck contained sad details of life on board. Seven messmates would have used these wooden spoons to eat their meals of porridge from a single shared bowl. Officers ate from pewter plates.

Traces of red paint can be seen on the jaws

SUNKEN GRAVEYARD
Divers found 25 skeletons in or near the *Vasa* when they began to explore the wreck. Many lay where they had fallen at the time of the sinking – one man was trapped under a heavy gun carriage. Divers also retrieved clothes and shoes with the bodies of the seamen. The coldness of the northern harbour, and the low salt content of the Baltic Sea, had prevented the fabrics and leathers from rotting. As well as the garments that the seamen were wearing, some had a change of clothes packed in wooden chests on the decks where they lived, worked, and slept.

SKELETON CREW
The full crew would have numbered 145, and the ship would also have been carrying 300 soldiers. But there was a reduced crew of 100 for the maiden voyage, as well as some wives and children. The sinking drowned at least 50 people. Even the admiral had a narrow escape. The disaster would have been very much worse, however, if the *Vasa* had actually gone to sea.

TAKE A BOW

The discovery of the *Vasa* put an end to arguments about how shipwrights built 17th-century warships. Especially controversial was the ship's beak – the pointed section sticking out at the bow, with the figurehead at its tip. Oil paintings of the time showed warships with huge ornamental beaks, but many maritime experts believed that the artists had exaggerated their size. The discovery of the *Vasa* proved that the experts were wrong. After the ship had been reconstructed, she really did have a gigantic beak, decorated with carvings of 20 Roman emperors on parade.

Beakhead

DISCOVERY AND RAISING OF THE VASA

It was Swedish engineer and naval historian Anders Franzén (born 1918) who discovered the *Vasa* in 1956. A diver confirmed the location, and Franzén began a campaign to raise the wreck. Divers passed lifting cables under the hull, and salvage ships then pulled on the cables to raise the *Vasa* to the surface. Blocking the gunports and other holes in the ship's hull made it watertight, and once pumps had removed the water inside, the *Vasa* floated again.

SINKING SCULPTURE

To decorate the *Vasa*, woodcarvers sculpted 500 figures and 200 other ornaments from oak, pine, and lime woods. Mostly they chose mythical beasts, historical personalities, and Bible stories as their subjects. But they also carved mermaids, which superstitious seamen believed would protect them on a voyage. Unfortunately, the reverse was true. The weight of the many carvings almost certainly made the *Vasa* more top-heavy, and helped to capsize the ship.

Golden-brown paint still visible on the lion's mane

ROYAL CREST

The Swedish national emblem decorated the stern of the *Vasa*. Carvers built it from 22 separate pieces. Like many other carvings fixed to the ship, the crest still had traces of the golden-brown paint that once made it gleam majestically.

GLOOMY GUN DECK

The lower gun deck of the *Vasa*, with its low beams and dark timbers, was completely reconstructed. Conservators replaced the gun carriages where they were found, but 17th-century salvage divers removed the guns that they once supported.

"Unsinkable" Titanic

ICEBERGS MAKE THE NORTH ATLANTIC a fearsome obstacle course in the spring. Some icebergs tower as high as office blocks above passing ships, but nine times as much ice floats unseen below the surface of the sea. Passengers on the *Titanic*'s maiden (first) voyage in April 1912 had no reason to fear icebergs. Everyone thought the *Titanic* was the safest ocean liner in the world – it was certainly the largest and most luxurious. Sadly, it was not "unsinkable", as the passengers believed. In the middle of the night, on the 15th April, an iceberg buckled the steel hull of the *Titanic* below the water-line. Sea water rushed in and the ship sunk in three hours. More than 1,500 people died in the world's most notorious shipwreck.

LAUNCHING A DOOMED MONSTER
The *Titanic* was built in Belfast, Northern Ireland in 26 months. The ship was launched on 31st May, 1911. To make it as safe as possible, the ship's hull was divided into watertight compartments. Even if a hole allowed two compartments to fill with sea water the *Titanic* would still float, but the iceberg that sank it holed five compartments.

FASTEST HOTEL AFLOAT
Even though the *Titanic* was one of the fastest liners afloat, the trip across the Atlantic took more than four days. Passengers travelled in surroundings as comfortable as any good hotel.

WRECK OF THE TITANIC
The *Titanic* broke in two and sank in 3,800 m (12,470 ft) of water – well beyond the reach of divers. The wreck was lost until 1985, when a vessel from Woods Hole Oceanographic Institution in the United States found it using the remote-controlled submersible *Argo*. Modelmakers created this reconstruction of the wreck from photographs and video footage taken by the submersible.

TELEGRAPH OPERATOR
Wireless operator Jack Phillips was so busy sending passengers' messages that he interrupted an ice warning from a nearby ship in order to continue transmission. When the *Titanic* began to sink, however, Phillips' SOS signals (p. 36) summoned help quickly. The *Titanic* disaster proved the value of radio in life-saving at sea, and soon all ships carried the equipment.

TOO FEW BOATS
Although the *Titanic* could carry 3,547 people, there was space in the lifeboats for only a third of them. As a result of the wreck, international shipping laws changed, forcing vessels to provide lifeboat space for every single passenger and crew member.

Bitts (bollards), for attaching cables, still stand on the deck

FRENCH SUPER-SUB
In 1987 a French team sailed to the *Titanic* shipwreck. Using the mechanical arms of the submarine, *Nautile*, its crew lifted hundreds of objects. Survivors of the wreck and relatives of the dead attacked the expedition as sinister souvenir hunting.

ON DECK
The coldness of the Atlantic water did not protect the *Titanic* from damage, as many had hoped it would. Marine worms have consumed most of the ship's ornate woodwork, and rust hangs in festoons from steel equipment.

Deck has collapsed where elegant glass dome once stood

Gate still closed between third-class and first-class areas

WINDOW ON A WRECK
The Woods Hole team returned in 1986 and dived to the *Titanic* in the deep-sea submersible, *Alvin*. Cameras on board photographed much of the wreck, including this stateroom window.

Cargo crane

BURIED BOW
The ship's bow sank fast enough to plough itself 18 m (60 ft) deep into the seabed, and this deck rail now lies only a little way out of the mud. Concretions (p. 56) on deck equipment have made them resemble a figurehead, though the *Titanic* did not carry one.

Anchor crane

Oil tanker disasters

THE SHIPS THAT CARRY OIL are the biggest in the world, and their size makes them difficult to control. A ship needs several times its own length to turn, and oil tankers can be as long as 20 tennis courts. If they run aground, crude (unrefined) oil is often spilt. The oil floats on the surface of the water forming a slick – a black, tarry layer. A slick coats everything it touches, polluting beaches and covering sea birds and mammals. The biggest tankers carry enough oil to fill 300 full-length swimming pools. Risking a spill of this size perhaps seems like gambling with the environment, but without their vital cargoes our cars would stop and we would shiver in cold homes. To reduce the danger, new tankers must now be fitted with a double skin (a hull within a hull).

STRANDED TANKER
When the engines of the *Braer* failed in January 1993, the tanker drifted helplessly. Heavy seas prevented tugs from towing the *Braer* to safety. The tanker ran aground on the jagged rocks of Scotland's Shetland isle.

ALASKAN SPILL
Pumping out oil from the grounded *Exxon Valdez* tanker helped to limit the damage to Alaska's coastline in 1989. The cleanup operation was problematic because of freezing temperatures and the site's remoteness, and one-sixth of the cargo – 42 million litres (9.2 million gallons) – escaped anyway. The spill seems huge, but industries and refineries in the United States consume this quantity of oil every 22 seconds.

CONTAINING THE SLICK
Oil coats only the surface of water, so it is possible to prevent a slick from spreading by blocking its path with a boom (long floating barrier). Workers in Wales launched a boom to contain the slick that spread from the *Sea Empress*, after it ran aground in 1996.

TANKER INFERNO
When a tanker runs aground and cannot be refloated, pollution experts first try to pump oil from its tanks. If this is impossible, they may consider setting light to the tanker deliberately to burn off the oil. Fires also start accidentally, though all tankers have fire control systems to prevent this. Tankers make easy targets during wars, and burning them deprives an enemy of vital supplies.

BEACH HOSES
Washing oiled beaches with high-pressure hoses forces some of the oil back into the sea, where it is easier to scoop up. This makes the sand look clean, but some experts believe that it prolongs pollution by driving the oil deeper into the beach.

OILED BIRDS
Spilled oil quickly covers the plumage of the marine birds that swim on the ocean and feed on the fish that live in it. The oil clogs up the bird's feathers, weighing them down and leaving them unable to fly. Birds peck at their feathers to clean themselves, and the oil that they swallow as a result may poison them.

BIRD BATHS
Capturing oiled birds and washing their feathers with detergents helps to remove the oil. When they have recovered, the birds are released. However, experts disagree about the effectiveness of cleaning. Recent research suggests that many birds die within a few weeks of release.

THE COAST IS CLEAR
The ocean environment gradually cleans itself after an oil spill. About a third of the oil evaporates within two days. Waves and sunlight eventually break the remainder into tiny drops that microorganisms can destroy. Cleaned mammals and birds, such as these penguins, can return to the wild within months of a spill.

COASTAL CLEANING
Cleaning an oiled coastline can be an enormous task. When the tanker *Exxon Valdez* ran aground on Alaska's Bligh Reef in 1989, its cargo polluted 2,000 km (1,250 miles) of coast. As many as 11,000 people helped to repair the damage. One of their tasks was to remove pebbles one-by-one for hot-water washing.

Navigation

THE FIRST SAILORS NAVIGATED by following the coastline. This was slow, however, and rocks or shallows were never far away. When mariners sailed out of sight of land some 4,500 years ago they followed stars, or the wind's direction – the compass was not invented until the 12th century. Sailors calculated distance from their speed and sailing time. Drawing charts and maps also helped them navigate. These methods, however, were not precise enough to avoid wrecking on the most distant shores. So navigators learned to judge latitude (how far north or south they sailed) by measuring the Sun's position. A simple way of finding a ship's position in an east-west direction (longitude) was invented in 1761.

Mirror reflects Sun

Telescope magnifies image of Sun and horizon

Ship's captain using a sextant

Lower mirror is half-silvered, so horizon is visible

LATITUDE CALCULATOR
Invented in 1757, the sextant enabled sailors to determine latitude (their position north or south of the equator). By looking into the eyepiece of the sextant's telescope, a navigator can find the Sun's position relative to the horizon. Printed tables convert this into latitude.

Index bar

GUIDED BY THE SUN
As long ago as 300 BC, Greek astronomers knew that sundials cast longer shadows the further they are from the equator. Seamen of later ages used this information to estimate their position. In the 14th century they began to use instruments such as the astrolabe (p. 33) to measure the Sun's height more accurately.

The shadow vane slid across the scale, indicating Sun's altitude

Backsight was aligned with the horizon slit to give the estimated latitude

BACKSTAFF
The backstaff, invented by English navigator John Davis, in 1595, was a great improvement on the astrolabe (p. 33). To use it, the navigator stood with his back to the Sun and lined up the backsight and the horizon slit. The shadow vane was adjusted until the shadow fell on the horizon slit. The reading on the shadow vane was then added to the backsight reading to give the ship's true latitude.

Horizon slit

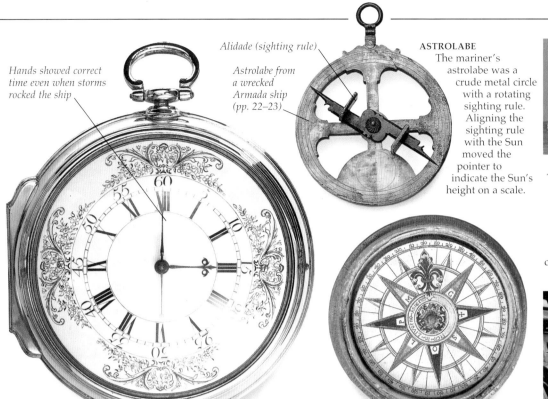

Hands showed correct time even when storms rocked the ship

Alidade (sighting rule)

Astrolabe from a wrecked Armada ship (pp. 22–23)

ASTROLABE
The mariner's astrolabe was a crude metal circle with a rotating sighting rule. Aligning the sighting rule with the Sun moved the pointer to indicate the Sun's height on a scale.

GUIDING BEACON
The invention of radio at the end of the 19th century allowed seafarers to receive warnings of bad weather or icebergs. By the 1950s chains of radio beacons began to broadcast signals purely for navigation. By comparing signals from two beacons, navigators could calculate exactly where they were.

RADAR STEERING
Radar helps to guide mariners in the dark or fog. The equipment broadcasts a radio signal and measures the strength of echoes. Radar screens show nearby ships, buoys, or coastlines as bright shapes.

CLOCKS SHOW THE WAY
In 1759 English clockmaker John Harrison built a chronometer that measured time accurately enough for navigation. The Sun rises two seconds later each day for each kilometre (0.6 mile) that mariners sail west, so the change in time when the Sun is directly overhead is a precise way to calculate longitude.

MAGNETIC MIRACLE
Balanced on a central pivot, or floating in liquid, the magnetized needle at the heart of a compass always turns to point north. Chinese navigators were the first to guide their ships with the aid of a compass around 1100.

ON THE BRIDGE
Around the wheel of a modern ship are radar screens, computerized charts, and other navigational aids. A receiver for signals from global positioning satellites (GPS) gives the helmsman accurate readouts of the ship's position.

Computerized chart plotter

GPS receiver

Echo-sounder

Radar screen

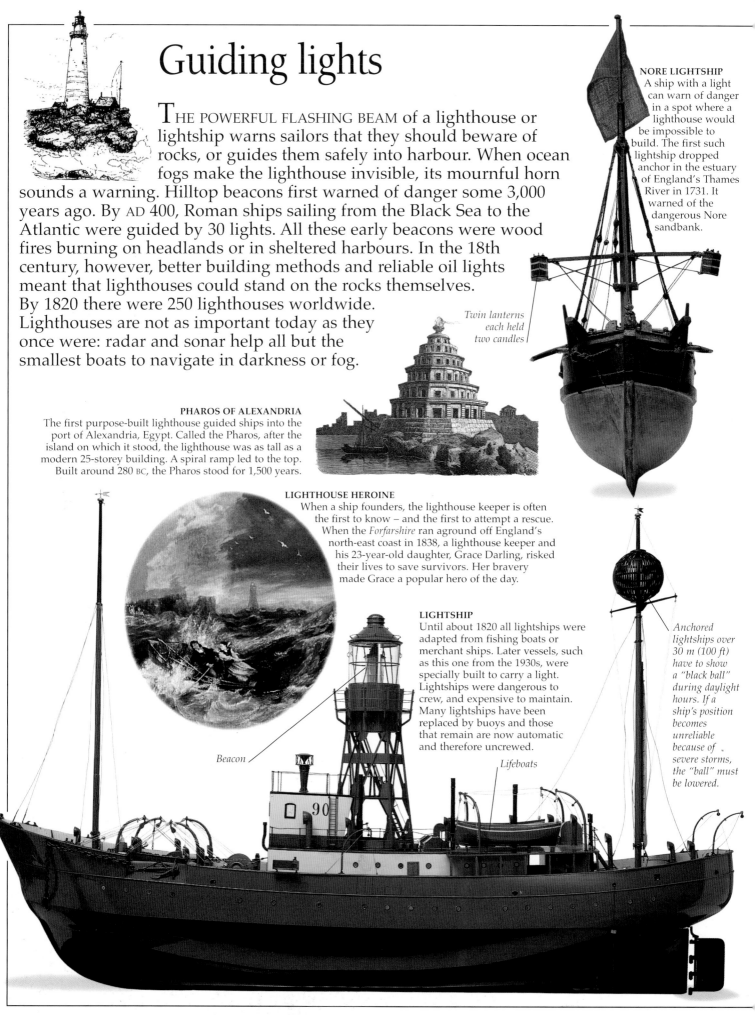

Guiding lights

THE POWERFUL FLASHING BEAM of a lighthouse or lightship warns sailors that they should beware of rocks, or guides them safely into harbour. When ocean fogs make the lighthouse invisible, its mournful horn sounds a warning. Hilltop beacons first warned of danger some 3,000 years ago. By AD 400, Roman ships sailing from the Black Sea to the Atlantic were guided by 30 lights. All these early beacons were wood fires burning on headlands or in sheltered harbours. In the 18th century, however, better building methods and reliable oil lights meant that lighthouses could stand on the rocks themselves. By 1820 there were 250 lighthouses worldwide. Lighthouses are not as important today as they once were: radar and sonar help all but the smallest boats to navigate in darkness or fog.

Twin lanterns each held two candles

NORE LIGHTSHIP
A ship with a light can warn of danger in a spot where a lighthouse would be impossible to build. The first such lightship dropped anchor in the estuary of England's Thames River in 1731. It warned of the dangerous Nore sandbank.

PHAROS OF ALEXANDRIA
The first purpose-built lighthouse guided ships into the port of Alexandria, Egypt. Called the Pharos, after the island on which it stood, the lighthouse was as tall as a modern 25-storey building. A spiral ramp led to the top. Built around 280 BC, the Pharos stood for 1,500 years.

LIGHTHOUSE HEROINE
When a ship founders, the lighthouse keeper is often the first to know – and the first to attempt a rescue. When the *Forfarshire* ran aground off England's north-east coast in 1838, a lighthouse keeper and his 23-year-old daughter, Grace Darling, risked their lives to save survivors. Her bravery made Grace a popular hero of the day.

LIGHTSHIP
Until about 1820 all lightships were adapted from fishing boats or merchant ships. Later vessels, such as this one from the 1930s, were specially built to carry a light. Lightships were dangerous to crew, and expensive to maintain. Many lightships have been replaced by buoys and those that remain are now automatic and therefore uncrewed.

Anchored lightships over 30 m (100 ft) have to show a "black ball" during daylight hours. If a ship's position becomes unreliable because of severe storms, the "ball" must be lowered.

Beacon

Lifeboats

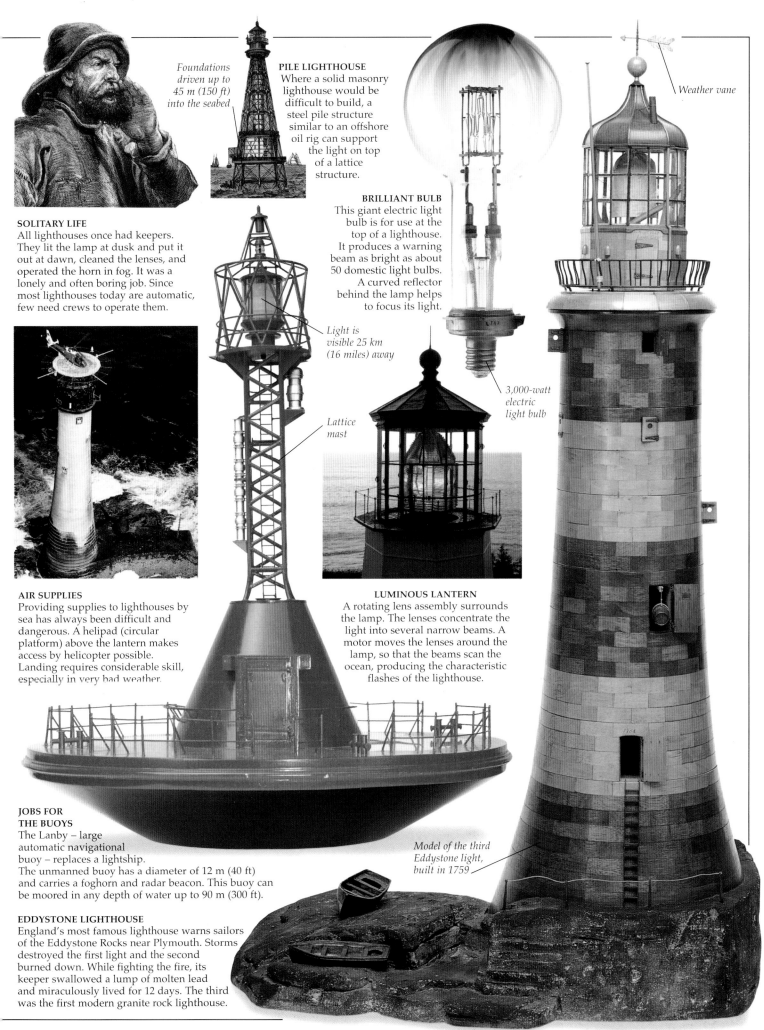

PILE LIGHTHOUSE
Where a solid masonry lighthouse would be difficult to build, a steel pile structure similar to an offshore oil rig can support the light on top of a lattice structure.

Foundations driven up to 45 m (150 ft) into the seabed

SOLITARY LIFE
All lighthouses once had keepers. They lit the lamp at dusk and put it out at dawn, cleaned the lenses, and operated the horn in fog. It was a lonely and often boring job. Since most lighthouses today are automatic, few need crews to operate them.

BRILLIANT BULB
This giant electric light bulb is for use at the top of a lighthouse. It produces a warning beam as bright as about 50 domestic light bulbs. A curved reflector behind the lamp helps to focus its light.

Weather vane

Light is visible 25 km (16 miles) away

Lattice mast

3,000-watt electric light bulb

AIR SUPPLIES
Providing supplies to lighthouses by sea has always been difficult and dangerous. A helipad (circular platform) above the lantern makes access by helicopter possible. Landing requires considerable skill, especially in very bad weather.

LUMINOUS LANTERN
A rotating lens assembly surrounds the lamp. The lenses concentrate the light into several narrow beams. A motor moves the lenses around the lamp, so that the beams scan the ocean, producing the characteristic flashes of the lighthouse.

JOBS FOR THE BUOYS
The Lanby – large automatic navigational buoy – replaces a lightship. The unmanned buoy has a diameter of 12 m (40 ft) and carries a foghorn and radar beacon. This buoy can be moored in any depth of water up to 90 m (300 ft).

Model of the third Eddystone light, built in 1759

EDDYSTONE LIGHTHOUSE
England's most famous lighthouse warns sailors of the Eddystone Rocks near Plymouth. Storms destroyed the first light and the second burned down. While fighting the fire, its keeper swallowed a lump of molten lead and miraculously lived for 12 days. The third was the first modern granite rock lighthouse.

Communications

I require assistance

Rocks ahead

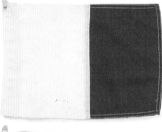

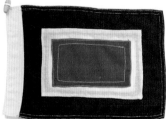

You are steering towards
the centre of a typhoon

TALKING FLAGS
Flag signalling is an ancient art, but in the 19th century the introduction of a standard code helped mariners make better use of them. The code book, published worldwide, gave the meaning of thousands of flag combinations. To save time, urgent messages use the fewest flags.

BY SIGNALLING WITH FLAGS, lights, sound, or radio, the crew of a crippled ship can summon help, or warn vessels of unseen danger. Emergency communications are so vital that mariners of all nations have agreed standard distress calls. Radio operators tune their sets to a frequency reserved for emergency signals, and broadcast "Mayday". This word is based on "m'aidez", which means "help me" in French. In Morse code the distress signal is "SOS", a meaningless set of letters chosen because they are easy to send, and rarely occur together in a normal message. Modern rescue beacons broadcast automatically, but sailors still learn the traditional distress signals, since their lives may depend on them.

SEMAPHORE SIGNALLING
When naval ships were close enough, their crews signalled with hand flags. The British semaphore system indicated letters by the angles of two flags. In American wigwag code, the waving of a single flag communicated the message.

READING THE SIGNS
The sailor's nickname for a telescope – "bring-'em-near" – wittily describes what it did for flag signals, making them many times easier to read.

Table of signalling flags

Eyepiece

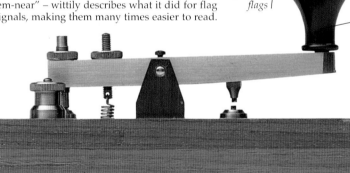

Morse code sending key

TAPPING OUT THE MESSAGE
By tapping a key such as this, radio operators could broadcast the alphabet in a code of long and short pulses, known as Morse code. When Samuel Morse devised the code in 1838, 50 years before the invention of radio, it was communicated using signalling lamps – a method still widely used at sea.

Horn produces loud blast of air

Bellows

NOISY BOX
In fog, steamships avoided collisions by blowing their horns or whistles. On sailing ships a hand-powered foghorn blew out a warning loud enough to be heard 1.6 km (1 mile) away. Winding a handle gradually filled the bellows with air, which was then discharged through the horn in a deafening blast.

MECHANICAL SEMAPHORE

French engineer Claude Chappé invented a visual telegraph in 1794. At the top of a tall mast, the position of its adjustable arms represented the letters of the alphabet. Variations of Chappé's telegraph transmitted two or three letters a minute.

Eyepiece

Shutter trigger

ALDIS LAMP

The invention of the electric light made signalling lamps more powerful. Inventor Arthur Aldis perfected the lamp named after him. Its trigger-operated shutter flashed the light more rapidly than a switch.

On/off lamp trigger

Clapper

A VERY GOOD IDEA

A distress rocket or flare is visible even when waves hide the ship that fired it. United States naval officer Edward Very (1847–1910) devised a pistol to fire them high into the sky. Modern rockets do not need a separate firing mechanism.

Pistol opened like an ordinary gun

WEBLEY & SCOTT Lᵀᴰ LONDON & BIRMINGHAM

Body (frame)

Stock (grip)

Cartridge fitted into wide barrel

RINGING OUT A WARNING

In fog a ship's bell gave an audible warning of its position, but sound is a poor way of sending more detailed signals. Strong wind, for instance, can drown out the sound of a bell. The bell also functioned as a clock during each four-hour watch on board ship, the bell being struck every half-hour of the watch.

Rope for ringing out a warning in fog, or for chiming the time

SIGNALLING LAMP

By flashing a light, ships several miles apart can communicate on a clear night. In 1867, British Admiral Philip Colomb suggested using a code of long and short flashes. Morse code replaced Colomb's shortly afterwards.

WIRELESS COMMUNICATION

The invention of radio in 1895 provided a powerful new way of communicating. Ships were quick to take advantage of "wireless telegraphy", especially after the *Titanic* disaster (pp. 28–29) proved its life-saving value.

Sailor signals to distant ships in Morse code

Shipwreck survivors

THOSE WHO ESCAPE SINKING SHIPS celebrate their good luck only briefly, for their ordeal has only just begun. The obvious danger they face is drowning, but cold seas can also kill in minutes. Liferafts provide protection against both, but perhaps the cruellest hazard of all is thirst. Sea water is everywhere, but it contains salt and drinking it makes the body dehydrated. When fresh water runs out, it is better to drink nothing, and wait for rain. Thirst may torture survivors, but it will not kill them for two weeks – if they can avoid the moisture loss caused by sweating. Food is surprisingly unimportant, but shelter is crucial: sunlight consumes vital water and burns and blisters skin. Suffering these hazards has driven shipwrecked mariners mad, but those who are determined enough to endure them have been rescued after more than four months at sea.

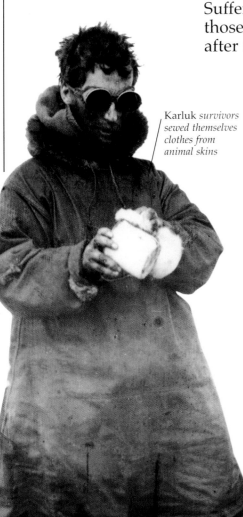

Karluk survivors sewed themselves clothes from animal skins

RAFT OF THE CANNIBALS
When the French ship *Medusa* ran aground off Africa's coast in July 1816, passengers and crew huddled aboard a makeshift raft. While it drifted for 12 days, all but 15 died or were killed in fights. Survivors lived off the flesh of the dead. The affair shocked French people even before Théodore Géricault (1791–1824) completed this painting of their ordeal in 1819.

LIFE-SAVING RECLINER
Ordinary wooden lifeboats need launching by experienced crew – perhaps when a ship is sinking and the passengers are panicking. Deck-seat rafts, by contrast, drift free as the ship sinks, or can simply be thrown into the water. The most basic are little more than large floats, but this deck-seat lifeboat provided a little more protection to those on board.

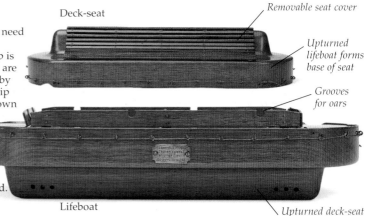

Deck-seat

Removable seat cover

Upturned lifeboat forms base of seat

Grooves for oars

Lifeboat

Upturned deck-seat forms a lifeboat

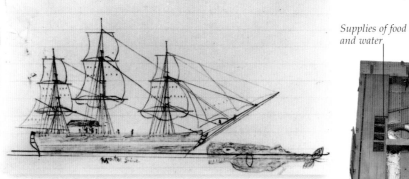

WHALE WRECK
When a whale rammed the *Essex* in the Pacific Ocean in 1820, the crew escaped in rowing boats. Some survived for three months, tortured by storms, sharks, and hunger. They ate the bodies of those who died, then killed and ate Owen Coffin, the cabin boy. American author Herman Melville made the story famous in his novel *Moby Dick*.

KARLUK SURVIVORS
When Arctic ice trapped his ship, the *Karluk*, in 1913, Canadian explorer Vilhjalmur Stefansson took off with the best dogs and a few crew members. The abandoned crew survived for nearly a year on an Arctic island after pack ice (p. 11) crushed the ship. The *Karluk's* captain travelled 1,125 km (700 m) to get help, but many crew members had died of cold, suicide, and disease before rescuers found them. Stefansson was presumed dead but turned up in 1918, having survived for five years in the Arctic.

Supplies of food and water

20-30 survivors shared raft

CHIPCHASE LIFERAFT
The danger of torpedoes in World War II forced crews to abandon ship quickly. A quick-release mechanism sent the wooden Chipchase raft sliding down its launch ramp into the sea.

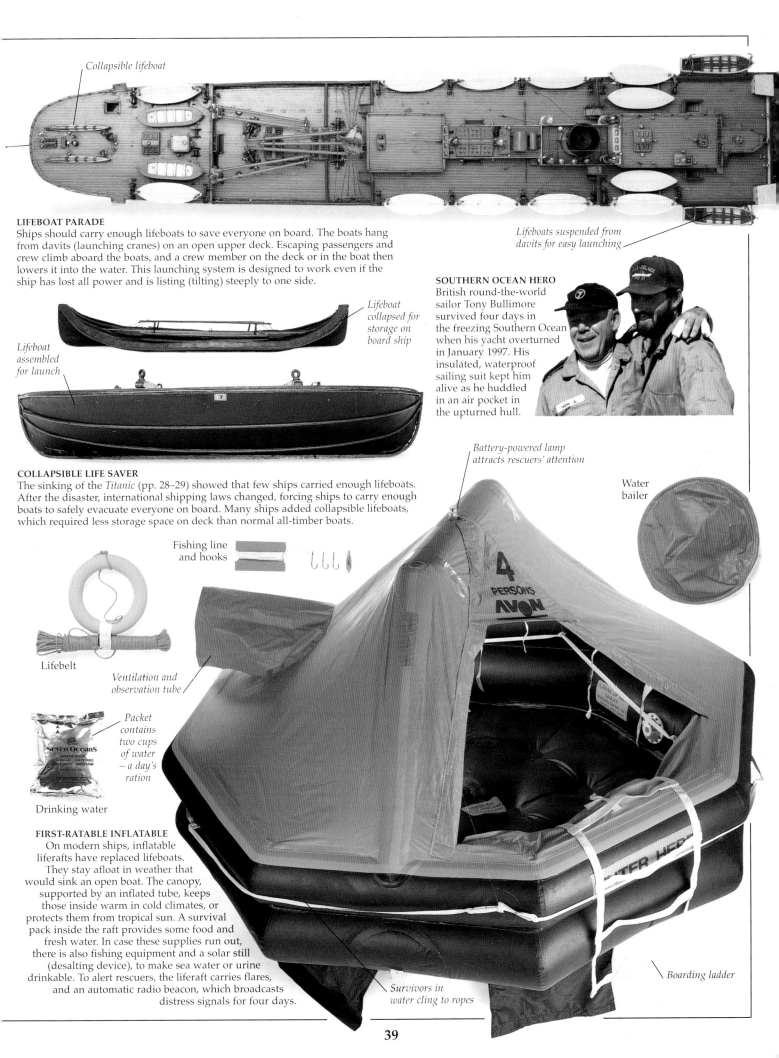

Collapsible lifeboat

Lifeboats suspended from davits for easy launching

LIFEBOAT PARADE

Ships should carry enough lifeboats to save everyone on board. The boats hang from davits (launching cranes) on an open upper deck. Escaping passengers and crew climb aboard the boats, and a crew member on the deck or in the boat then lowers it into the water. This launching system is designed to work even if the ship has lost all power and is listing (tilting) steeply to one side.

Lifeboat collapsed for storage on board ship

Lifeboat assembled for launch

SOUTHERN OCEAN HERO

British round-the-world sailor Tony Bullimore survived four days in the freezing Southern Ocean when his yacht overturned in January 1997. His insulated, waterproof sailing suit kept him alive as he huddled in an air pocket in the upturned hull.

COLLAPSIBLE LIFE SAVER

The sinking of the *Titanic* (pp. 28–29) showed that few ships carried enough lifeboats. After the disaster, international shipping laws changed, forcing ships to carry enough boats to safely evacuate everyone on board. Many ships added collapsible lifeboats, which required less storage space on deck than normal all-timber boats.

Battery-powered lamp attracts rescuers' attention

Water bailer

Fishing line and hooks

Lifebelt

Ventilation and observation tube

Packet contains two cups of water – a day's ration

Drinking water

FIRST-RATABLE INFLATABLE

On modern ships, inflatable liferafts have replaced lifeboats. They stay afloat in weather that would sink an open boat. The canopy, supported by an inflated tube, keeps those inside warm in cold climates, or protects them from tropical sun. A survival pack inside the raft provides some food and fresh water. In case these supplies run out, there is also fishing equipment and a solar still (desalting device), to make sea water or urine drinkable. To alert rescuers, the liferaft carries flares, and an automatic radio beacon, which broadcasts distress signals for four days.

Survivors in water cling to ropes

Boarding ladder

Air and sea rescues

W HEN A DISTRESS CALL SUMMONS LIFEBOAT CREWS, they do not waste a second. They jump into waterproof clothes and hurriedly board the rescue boat, for the slightest delay could mean lost lives. The vessel they launch is called a lifeboat, but it has little else in common with survival craft launched from sinking ships. These lifeboats are speedy and unsinkable, and specially built to search for, and rescue, mariners in distress. There are many different types, ranging from inshore inflatables to large offshore lifeboats that can answer distress calls up to 80 km (50 miles) away. Lifeboats cannot reach more distant emergencies quickly enough, so helicopters take their place.

LIFEBOAT PIONEER
The world's first national lifeboat service began in England in 1824. It was the creation of William Hillary (1771–1847), a lifeboat crewman on the Isle of Man, England. The Shipwreck Institution he founded is now called the Royal National Lifeboat Institution (RNLI).

Horse-drawn lifeboat

HORSES FOR COURSES
Lifeboats stationed on flat beaches may be far from the sea at low tide. Before they can launch the boat, the crew must take it to the water. In the past, a team of horses dragged the boat into the surf on a carriage. Now a tractor provides the power.

Greathead lifeboat

Cork flotation aids

SAFETY AT SEA
Early lifeboats did not sink in rough seas, but if they capsized they were difficult to turn the right way up. Self-righting designs, such as this 8.5-m (28-ft) rowing boat (left), appeared in the 1850s. Nevertheless, some lifeboat crews preferred traditional boats that were easier to handle and keep upright.

Trailer for launching lifeboat into the water

FIRST LIFEBOATS
Sea-faring folk have a long tradition of life-saving using ordinary boats. In the late 18th century, various inventors in Britain and France suggested adding iron keels and extra flotation to make these boats more suitable for rescue. This Greathead lifeboat, built in 1790, was among the first of the unsinkable designs.

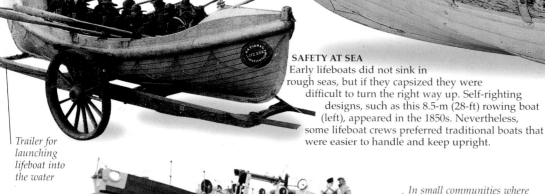

In small communities where no motorized transport existed lifeboats often had to be dragged some way before and after a rescue

HEAVE-HO!
Coastal communities have a special reason to support the work of lifeboats. Everybody has a relative or friend in the crew, and many of the rescues pluck local mariners and fishermen from the sea. So when a lifeboat needs hauling up the beach, everyone lends a hand.

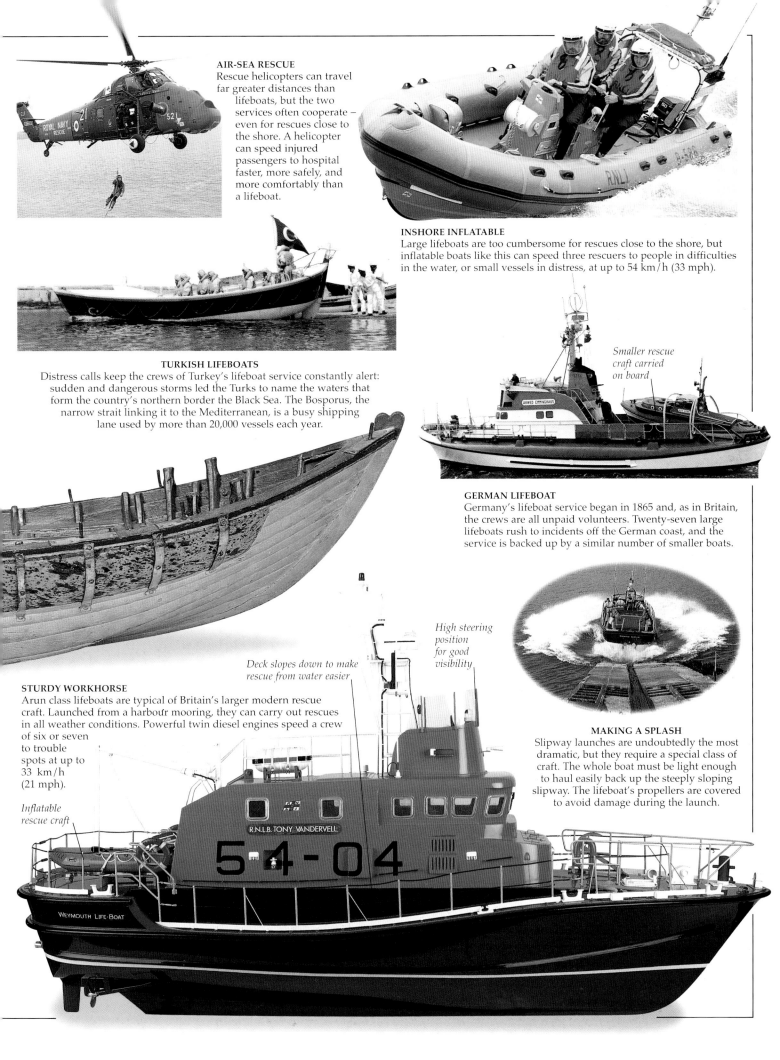

AIR-SEA RESCUE
Rescue helicopters can travel far greater distances than lifeboats, but the two services often cooperate – even for rescues close to the shore. A helicopter can speed injured passengers to hospital faster, more safely, and more comfortably than a lifeboat.

INSHORE INFLATABLE
Large lifeboats are too cumbersome for rescues close to the shore, but inflatable boats like this can speed three rescuers to people in difficulties in the water, or small vessels in distress, at up to 54 km/h (33 mph).

TURKISH LIFEBOATS
Distress calls keep the crews of Turkey's lifeboat service constantly alert: sudden and dangerous storms led the Turks to name the waters that form the country's northern border the Black Sea. The Bosporus, the narrow strait linking it to the Mediterranean, is a busy shipping lane used by more than 20,000 vessels each year.

Smaller rescue craft carried on board

GERMAN LIFEBOAT
Germany's lifeboat service began in 1865 and, as in Britain, the crews are all unpaid volunteers. Twenty-seven large lifeboats rush to incidents off the German coast, and the service is backed up by a similar number of smaller boats.

STURDY WORKHORSE
Arun class lifeboats are typical of Britain's larger modern rescue craft. Launched from a harbour mooring, they can carry out rescues in all weather conditions. Powerful twin diesel engines speed a crew of six or seven to trouble spots at up to 33 km/h (21 mph).

Inflatable rescue craft

Deck slopes down to make rescue from water easier

High steering position for good visibility

MAKING A SPLASH
Slipway launches are undoubtedly the most dramatic, but they require a special class of craft. The whole boat must be light enough to haul easily back up the steeply sloping slipway. The lifeboat's propellers are covered to avoid damage during the launch.

R.N.L.B. TONY VANDERVELL

5 4 - 0 4

WEYMOUTH LIFE-BOAT

Lifeboat equipment

IN THE BRIDGE, OR WHEELHOUSE, of a modern lifeboat, computers and radio equipment help the crew to speed towards vessels in distress. Automatic navigation systems pinpoint the lifeboat's location with the aid of radio signals from satellites and coastal beacons. A computerized chart plotter shows the surrounding coastline, buoys, and hazards. An echo-sounder measures water depth. Radio equipment allows the crew to keep in touch with other rescue services, and with the vessel in trouble. For the rescue itself, though, equipment has changed little in 50 years. Below are some of the tools and tackle that lifeboats carry, but one important detail is missing – the bravery of the volunteer crew is the most vital equipment of all, for without it every rescue attempt would fail.

PRACTICE MAKES PERFECT
There is no substitute for hands-on rescue experience, but lifeboat crews need first-aid training so they can treat casualties safely. Other courses teach skills in the use of radar and radio equipment.

BOATHOOK
With the help of a boathook, rescuers can pull a small crippled vessel alongside the lifeboat, or hold on to someone floating in the water.

Rope is fired from this end

SPEEDLINE DEVICE
Pulling the trigger fires a rocket that carries a line of rope a distance of 230 m (755 ft).

Cordage (rope)

HAND-HELD FLARES
Flares that produce a brilliant red flame or a plume of orange smoke are used to catch the attention of other rescuers.

Trigger for firing rope

ROPE AND PULLEY
Threading a rope through a block and tackle (pulley) makes a life buoy easier to recover from water.

Block and tackle

— *Nozzle*

FIRE FIGHTING
When going alongside a burning vessel, the crew protects the lifeboat from the flames by dousing it with water from a fire hose. A portable fire extinguisher is used to tackle any small fires on board the lifeboat.

Fire hose

Portable fire extinguisher

BILGE PUMP
Small enough to carry on to a waterlogged pleasure craft, this hand pump quickly drains the bilges (the lowest part of the hull) so that the boat floats higher in the water.

ANCHOR AND CHAIN
In shallow water, the anchor stops a lifeboat drifting, and keeps its bow headed into the waves.

FIRST-AID KIT
People rescued from the sea often need treatment for hypothermia (low body temperature). The crew use the first-aid kit to stabilize other injuries, such as burns and broken bones, until they can get the casualty to a doctor.

Headrest

Straps
for
securing
casualty

**BASKET
STRETCHER**
This stretcher
holds
casualties
securely for
transfer to a
helicopter or
lifeboat. Straps
prevent
movement,
which might
make any
injuries worse.

LIFE JACKET
Auto-inflated
life jackets keep
the wearer's
head above
water. Strong
straps allow
rescuers to lift a
colleague out of
the water
more easily.

LIFE BUOY
Survivors float inside life
buoys until rescuers arrive
to winch them to safety
with a system of ropes
and pulleys.

Rope for rescuers
to hoist survivor
out of the water

DROGUE
Dragging in the water, a
drogue (canvas bucket)
stops a vessel caught in
a gale from drifting,
and prevents waves
from breaking
dangerously
over the stern.

Whistle

Manually
activated
light

WINCH AWAY!
Straps on the basket
stretcher keep it level at the
end of a helicopter winch
cable. The winch operator,
who supervises the lift,
communicates with the
helicopter pilot by radio
and with hand signals.

Early diving

VALUABLE CARGOES have always lured swimmers brave enough to dive down to explore sunken wrecks. In Ancient Greece divers kept a third of the value of anything that they recovered from wrecks 3.7 m (12 ft) down; their share increased to half for wrecks twice as deep. Few people, however, can hold their breath for longer than two minutes and, as early as the 4th century BC, divers were carrying a supply of air trapped inside a barrel or a bell. In 1679, Italian scientist Giovanni Borelli (1608–1679) suggested prolonging dives by refreshing the air in the "diving bell" using a simple pump. For the next 250 years divers used pumped-air techniques to reach shipwrecks as deep as 60 m (200 ft).

Metal bands hold the wooden timbers firmly in place

BARREL DIVER
English diver John Lethbridge built one of the first really practical diving bells in 1715. Lowered on a rope to wrecks up to 9 m (30 ft) down, it contained enough air for half-an-hour's work. Wreck diving inside his barrel earned the inventor a fortune.

Simple signals were communicated to the surface by tugging on the rope

GLASS DIVING BELL
This fanciful picture shows Greek king, Alexander the Great (356–323 BC), as a diver. His glass diving bell would never have worked: water pressure would have crushed the glass and the lamps would have burned up all the oxygen.

COMMUNICATIONS BENEATH THE SEA
From about 1900, divers were able to communicate using microphones and small loudspeakers inside their helmets. Wire connected them to a miniature "telephone exchange" on the surface ship. The surface crew could listen to four divers at a time, flipping switches to talk to each in turn.

UNDERWATER BREATHING
Divers soon found alternatives to bells, but they continued to use the name for any kind of underwater chamber that held air. Helmets, with their thick glass window and pumped-air supply, enabled divers to make longer, more adventurous dives.

DIVE WEIGHTS
The air in divers' suits and helmets made them buoyant (lighter than water) so they floated. To descend to a wreck, divers strapped heavy lead weights over their suits.

Copper and brass helmet

CLOSED-CIRCUIT DIVING
The air that divers exhale contains carbon dioxide. By absorbing this poisonous gas, closed-circuit diving apparatus, such as this Italian mask from World War II, made the air fit for breathing again.

Pumped-air supply hose

Glass window

Straps attach mask to head

Twin-hose demand valve

Air supply gauge

END OF THE HOSE
The invention of the demand valve (p. 46) freed divers from cumbersome suits. Wearing compressed air cylinders on their backs and a mask, such as this 1950s example from Germany, they no longer had to rely on air pumped from the surface. This self-contained breathing apparatus (p. 46) enabled divers to descend safely to wrecks 50 m (165 ft) under water.

Rubber cuffs

AIRHEAD
An air hose and safety line linked a diver wearing a Siebe suit to the surface ship. There, a crew member operated a pump to force air down the tube and into the diver's helmet. The safety line was for raising the diver from the wreck, and for sending simple signals.

Layer of rubber sandwiched between canvas

SIEBE SUIT
In a heavy suit with a globe-like helmet, 19th-century divers could leave their diving bells and explore more freely. German watchmaker Augustus Siebe developed the first completely enclosed suit around 1830. For safety the Siebe helmets were sealed to the diver's waterproof suit. Earlier dive helmets were loose, and could fill with water if the diver fell.

Leather boots with lead bases to weigh down the diver

45

Scuba diving

To SWIM THROUGH A WRECK as free as a fish – this was always the dream of divers exploring the seabed. In 1943, French naval officer, Jacques Yves Cousteau, made the dream a reality. His aqualung used a novel regulator to control the pressure and flow of air from a cylinder on the diver's back. When the diver breathed in, the regulator opened to allow air to flow to the mouthpiece. The freedom of movement provided by the aqualung, or scuba (self-contained underwater breathing apparatus) diving equipment led to the discovery and exploration of many new wreck sites.

BUOYANCY CONTROL DEVICE
To swim effortlessly at a constant depth, divers wear inflatable jackets called buoyancy control devices (BCDs). Air in the lungs and suit gives divers positive buoyancy – they float. Weights give them negative buoyancy – they sink. By adjusting the amount of air in their BCDs, divers achieve neutral buoyancy – they move neither up nor down.

Air supply tube inflates BCD more quickly than the air from divers' lungs

Distress whistle for use on the surface of the water

Blowing air into mouthpiece inflates jacket

Reserve air tank

Demand valve on mouthpiece lets air flow when diver inhales

First stage on tank greatly reduces air pressure

Emergency mouthpiece, or octopus

UNDERWATER BREATHING APPARATUS
Carried on a harness on the diver's back, the underwater breathing apparatus draws air at high pressure from a large tank. Valves on top of the tank and on the mouthpieces reduce air pressure to the correct level for breathing.

Air tank

Compass

Depth gauge

Pressure gauge warns of low air supply

Dump valve for manual expulsion of air from the jacket

UNDERWATER VISION
Masks may leak under water, causing blurred vision. They are easily cleared, however, by tilting the head back and exhaling through the nose, so purging the mask.

Wet suit

Wave breaker

SNORKEL
Gripped in the mouth, a breathing tube, or snorkel, supplies air to a diver just below the surface of the water. Snorkels are short because water pressure makes breathing through them difficult in depths greater than 35 cm (14 in).

KITCHEN SINK INVENTORS
Jacques Cousteau (above) and engineer, Emile Gagnan, adapted the control valve of a gas cooker to equalize the pressure of the ocean with the pressure of the air breathed in by the diver. The new pressure regulator meant air could now be supplied on demand to a diver carrying a tank of compressed air on his back.

REEF EXPLORATION
Ships that run aground on coral reefs provide a perfect introduction to wreck diving. The tropical waters in which corals thrive are warm, shallow, and clear. Even if the wreck is impossible to find, the reef supports a huge variety of colourful and interesting sea life.

Removable weights

Quick-release clips

LIGHTING THE WAY
Since water absorbs light, the visibility under water is often very poor, especially on deep dives. An underwater torch can reveal unexpected colour in what looks like a dull scene and is an essential accessory on night dives.

WEIGHT BELT
Without weights, divers would float on the surface of the water, and would have to struggle to swim down to a wreck. In combination with a buoyancy jacket, the heavy lumps of metal give the diver neutral buoyancy. A quick-release buckle makes it easy to discard the belt in an emergency.

DIVING SUIT
A neoprene rubber wet suit prevents heat loss: in tropical waters a thinner suit protects against sunburn and stinging marine animals. Wet suits keep a layer of warm water against the body. Some divers prefer waterproof dry suits, under which warm clothes can be worn.

JET FINS
Like webbed feet, jet fins add power to a diver's swimming kicks. Open-heeled jet fins like these fit over the insulating boots that divers wear for warmth in cold water. Full-foot fins are more suitable for use with bare feet in warm water.

Boots keep the feet warm and prevent the fins from rubbing the skin

SAFETY KNIFE
A sharp dive knife is essential for cutting through fishing net or rope that can trap a diver under water. Dive knives have many other uses too: banging the handle on an air tank makes a loud sound, alerting nearby divers to danger.

Size and flexibility of fin must match diver's strength

Thick neoprene provides warmth and protection

Gloves

Deep-sea exploration

SINKING BELOW THE WAVES, wrecked ships slip out of sight – and perhaps out of reach. The ocean filters out the Sun's light and heat, leaving a cold, dark world. The deeper a wreck sinks, the more water presses down on it from above. Deep wreck sites are dangerous places for divers because the water pressure dissolves nitrogen gas in a diver's blood, causing narcosis – a kind of drunkenness. Divers must surface slowly, or risk developing decompression sickness (the bends) as the nitrogen forms bubbles in the veins. A wreck deeper than 100 m (330 ft) is beyond the reach of scuba divers, but in rigid suits divers can descend to 600 m (2,000 ft), while submarines can reach even deeper wrecks.

Suit was nicknamed "Jim" after Jim Jarrett who tested the prototype

PERESS SUIT
Inside a rigid atmospheric diving suit (ADS), the diver breathes air at atmospheric (normal) pressure, and can surface without having to enter a decompression chamber (right). In 1930 Joseph Peress developed one of the first successful ADS suits. Flexible joints in the arms and legs enabled the diver to move in depths up to 300 m (1,000 ft).

Ports on suit gave limited vision

Diver operated claws from inside the suit

DIVERS' DEN
To avoid the bends, divers enter a decompression chamber upon surfacing from deep dives. The chamber is filled with high-pressure air. As the pressure drops, excess nitrogen passes from the blood into the lungs, and is then exhaled safely.

DEEP WRECK
Using even the most sophisticated equipment, divers may have only a few minutes to investigate a deep wreck before their blood absorbs dangerous amounts of nitrogen.

ASHERAH SUBMERSIBLE
Techniques and equipment developed for deep dives can also be valuable aids in shallower water. In 1964, the University of Pennsylvania, USA, launched the first-ever submersible, *Asherah* – a submarine specially customized for underwater archaeology. Its first use was to survey a wreck at Yassi Ada, Turkey, in water 42 m (140 ft) deep. Led by George Bass, the first land archaeologist to study an underwater wreck, the team of two was able to map the site rapidly.

Frames form a ruled grid through which photographs of the wreck can be taken, and later pieced together to give an overall picture of the site

UNDERWATER BUBBLE
The crew of this modern submersible, *Remora*, can take it down to a wreck 600 m (2,000 ft) below the surface and explore the site for up to ten hours. The transparent bubble "cab" provides spectacular all-round views for the pilot and observer and, with the aid of thrusters (propellers), *Remora* is able to hover like a helicopter.

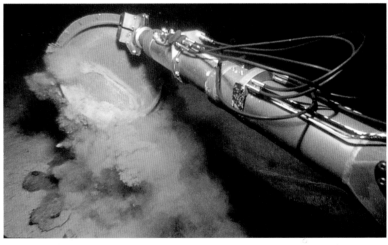

ARMS ACROSS THE OCEAN
Inside a submersible, the crew cannot reach out and touch the objects they see, like a free-swimming diver can. However, a jointed arm controlled from inside the vessel allows the crew to grip and retrieve loose artefacts from the wreck.

NEWT SUIT
ADS equipment is tiring for the operator inside, because at great depths the water pressure makes the suit stiffen. The fluid-filled joints of the Drager Newt Suit (left) reduce the problem, allowing divers roughly three-quarters of normal mobility. Despite this improvement, the suits are still cumbersome, though adding electric thrusters makes them easier to manoeuvre. Newt suits can reach wrecks 300 m (1,000 ft) down.

Wreck location and recovery

ONE OF THE MOST EFFECTIVE ways to locate a wreck is to ask fishermen where their nets get snagged! But a more systematic approach is to search dusty marine archives for the ship's last known position. If this reveals roughly where the wreck sank, technology can narrow the search. Sonar (sound navigation and ranging) surveys the contours of a wreck. Side-scan sonar (below) surveys large areas of the seabed using sound waves to produce a clearly definable "shadow" photograph. Magnetometers create magnetic maps of the seabed. These show the location of metal objects such as cannons – even if deep mud covers them. Marine archaeologists plan their dives using the charts that these instruments provide. Raising the wreck and cargo is obviously part of the task ahead. It is just as important, however, to record where each object rested. So before surfacing with their finds, divers spend much of their time under water measuring, mapping, sketching, and taking photographs.

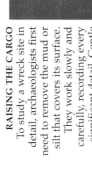

VIRTUAL AMPHORAE
To reconstruct *Arles IV*, a 1st-century AD wreck located off the southern French coast in 1981, technicians first made a mosaic of overlapping photographs from a height of 3 m (10 ft). They then used a computer to plot the contours, and created this digital 3-D image.

PLOTTING ARTEFACTS
A pre-disturbance survey is the first step of any archaeological investigation of a shipwreck. Divers make a grid, dividing the site exactly into squares using poles and wires. They can then record in which square each artefact lies, and measure its position within the square – including its depth below the grid. Finally, using photographs or sketches they collect enough data to map the site.

RAISING THE CARGO
To study a wreck site in detail, archaeologists first need to remove the mud or silt that covers its surface. They work slowly and carefully, recording every significant detail. Gentle fanning with the hand is often enough to remove soft silt. Heavier materials require powerful tools such as a propwash – a water jet that blows away mud. Once they have recorded finds, divers raise them with the help of an airlift – a buoyant, air-filled bag.

SIDEWAYS VIEW
Side-scan sonar mapping gives either a "broad view" of a wreck or a "close look". It reveals objects roughly 1/400th the size of the scan width, so to reveal an object as small as an amphora, the scan must be no wider than 400 amphorae.

STUDYING THE WRECK SITE
Sometimes scientists have their first view of the wreck without even having to get their feet wet. Cables carry signals from remote sensing devices, like sonar, up to a control room on the survey ship, where they appear on computer monitors or plotters.

Large anchor
provides a
clear marker
for this
wreck site

Diver surveys
a wreck before
beginning to
sketch the site

SEABED SURVEY

Pulled along under water at the end of a 400 m (1,310 ft) cable, the
cigar-shaped sonar "towfish" maps the seabed using "pings" of sound
waves. Sensors pick up echoes of the pulses, and the towfish transmits
them up a cable to the survey vessel for viewing and interpretation.

Life on board ship

"ABANDON SHIP!" When seafarers hear these dreaded words, they drop whatever they are doing and rush for their lives. There is rarely time to gather property – and rescue boats have no room for luggage. So countless personal possessions and everyday objects sink with the wreck. Carefully raised and documented, these items can provide a huge amount of information. Most objects are very ordinary, and nobody would call them sunken treasure, but to the marine archaeologist they can be worth more than a cargo of gold. The abandoned possessions of the crew give a vivid picture of what life was like on board ship. Tools and equipment may provide clues to the identity and date of a wreck. The location of these implements can also help archaeologists to assemble the jigsaw pieces of a wreck that has been broken up by fierce ocean currents.

COOKING UP A STORM
In storms, a fire on board simply added to the hazards, so a sailing ship's cook extinguished the stove and stowed away copper cooking pots. The crew lived on cold food until the weather improved.

PHARMACIST'S STOCK
Medical treatment was primitive in the age of sail, and more sailors died of disease than of drowning. The drugs that these bottles once contained were probably reserved for the officers. The ship that carried them, the *Earl of Abergavenny*, sank after running aground in February 1805.

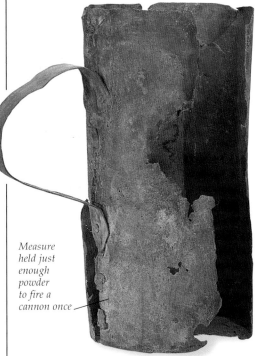

Measure held just enough powder to fire a cannon once

UNDERWATER WINE RACK
After just a few weeks at sea, drinking water became slimy and unpleasant, so every ship carried large quantities of wine, beer, and spirits. Careful packing gave protection against rough seas, and some bottles even survived a shipwreck.

EXPLOSIVE MEASURES
Warships had a magazine (storeroom) where gunpowder was measured out into silk bags. The discovery of a gunpowder measure, such as this one from the British flagship *Ramillies*, may pinpoint the location of the magazine.

GUN CARRIAGE
Wooden gun carriages did not float away from wrecks because the cannons they supported weighed them down. This carriage held a signalling gun about 1.2 m (4 ft) long.

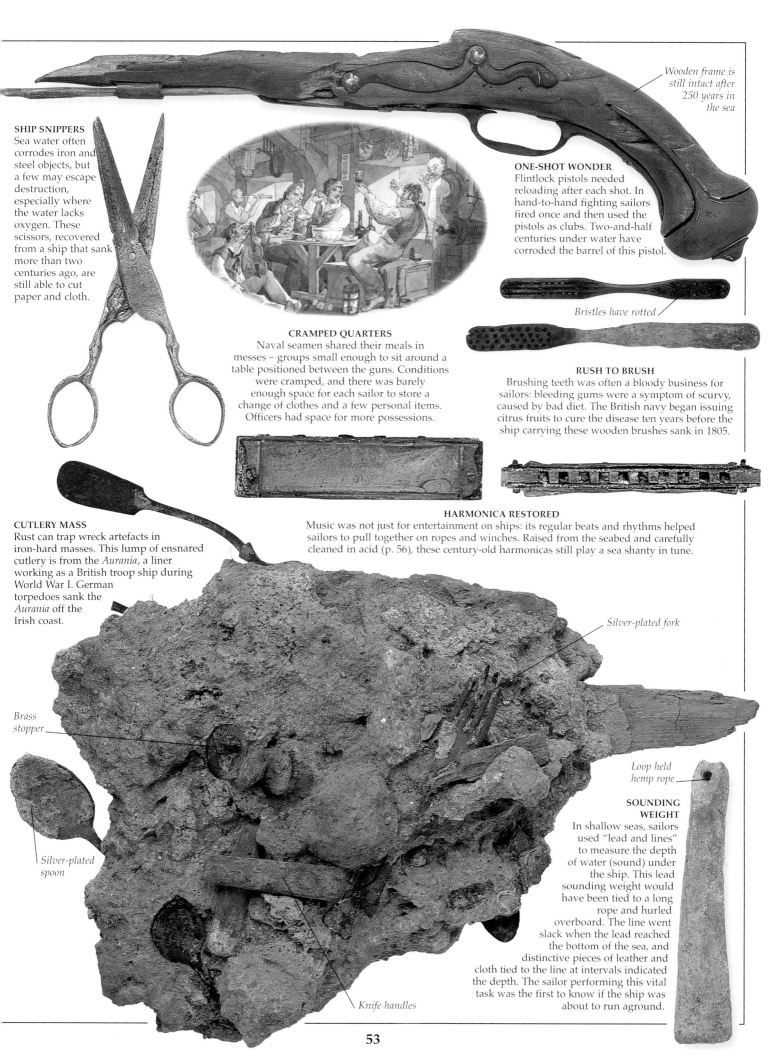

Wooden frame is still intact after 250 years in the sea

SHIP SNIPPERS
Sea water often corrodes iron and steel objects, but a few may escape destruction, especially where the water lacks oxygen. These scissors, recovered from a ship that sank more than two centuries ago, are still able to cut paper and cloth.

ONE-SHOT WONDER
Flintlock pistols needed reloading after each shot. In hand-to-hand fighting sailors fired once and then used the pistols as clubs. Two-and-half centuries under water have corroded the barrel of this pistol.

Bristles have rotted

CRAMPED QUARTERS
Naval seamen shared their meals in messes – groups small enough to sit around a table positioned between the guns. Conditions were cramped, and there was barely enough space for each sailor to store a change of clothes and a few personal items. Officers had space for more possessions.

RUSH TO BRUSH
Brushing teeth was often a bloody business for sailors: bleeding gums were a symptom of scurvy, caused by bad diet. The British navy began issuing citrus fruits to cure the disease ten years before the ship carrying these wooden brushes sank in 1805.

HARMONICA RESTORED
Music was not just for entertainment on ships: its regular beats and rhythms helped sailors to pull together on ropes and winches. Raised from the seabed and carefully cleaned in acid (p. 56), these century-old harmonicas still play a sea shanty in tune.

CUTLERY MASS
Rust can trap wreck artefacts in iron-hard masses. This lump of ensnared cutlery is from the *Aurania*, a liner working as a British troop ship during World War I. German torpedoes sank the *Aurania* off the Irish coast.

Silver-plated fork

Brass stopper

Silver-plated spoon

Loop held hemp rope

SOUNDING WEIGHT
In shallow seas, sailors used "lead and lines" to measure the depth of water (sound) under the ship. This lead sounding weight would have been tied to a long rope and hurled overboard. The line went slack when the lead reached the bottom of the sea, and distinctive pieces of leather and cloth tied to the line at intervals indicated the depth. The sailor performing this vital task was the first to know if the ship was about to run aground.

Knife handles

Lost cargoes

IN BUNDLES AND BALES, barrels, and boxes, cargo filled the holds of merchant ships. Its weight was essential to keep the ship upright during a voyage. In a wreck, however, a heavy cargo dragged the ship down. Bringing a cargo to the surface is called salvage. It is worthwhile only if the cargo is valuable and sea water has not harmed it. If a wreck can be identified, old documents can reveal what the hold contains in minute detail. Therefore, divers often know exactly what they are looking for – even where to find it. They do not always keep everything they bring to the surface, though. Salvage divers must pay the rightful owner a proportion of the value of everything recovered. Even if the wreck has rotted on the seabed for centuries, its cargo still belongs to someone.

COIN CACHE
Piled inside the remains of the hold, or scattered by the tides, coins are among the most common finds on wreck sites. Many ships carried currency and the metals from which coins are made do not corrode.

Spanish and American coin collection

Notes virtually unharmed after submersion in sea water

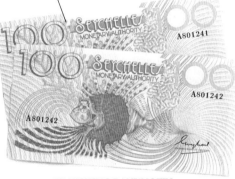

VANISHING BANKNOTES
Wrecked in 1979, the *Aeolian Sky* carried a fortune in Seychelles banknotes. By the time inspection divers reached the wreck, most of the money had been looted. The country's bank cancelled the issue, so these notes are now worthless.

REINDEER RECOVERED
Deep mud buried the wreck of the Danish ship *Die Fraumetta Catharina von Flensburg* when she sank in 1786. The mud preserved the ship's cargo of reindeer hides so well that they are still supple enough to make into clothing.

COPPER CARGO
Stowed very low in the hold, heavy cargo, such as these copper ingots, helped to stabilize the ship. Cast specially for the coppersmiths who worked in the bazaars of India, these ingots sank with the *Earl of Abergavenny* in 1805.

CASH ON THE MOVE
When the SS *Camberwell* struck a floating mine and sank in 1917, India was still a British colony, and its banknotes were printed in England. These ten-rupee notes were part of the ship's general cargo.

SEALED, NOT DELIVERED
The lead from which this seal was made is very resistant to sea water, so it survived long after the cloth it identified had rotted away. Markings show the length of the roll in ells. An ell varied from country to country – between 54 and 122 cm (21 and 48 in).

READY TO SAIL
Loading, or lading, a ship to make it ready for a voyage was a skilled task, for a cargo that shifted could cause a wreck. Seamen were superstitious about lading, and believed that a voyage would be successful only if the ship tilted to the port, or left, side as the cargo was loaded.

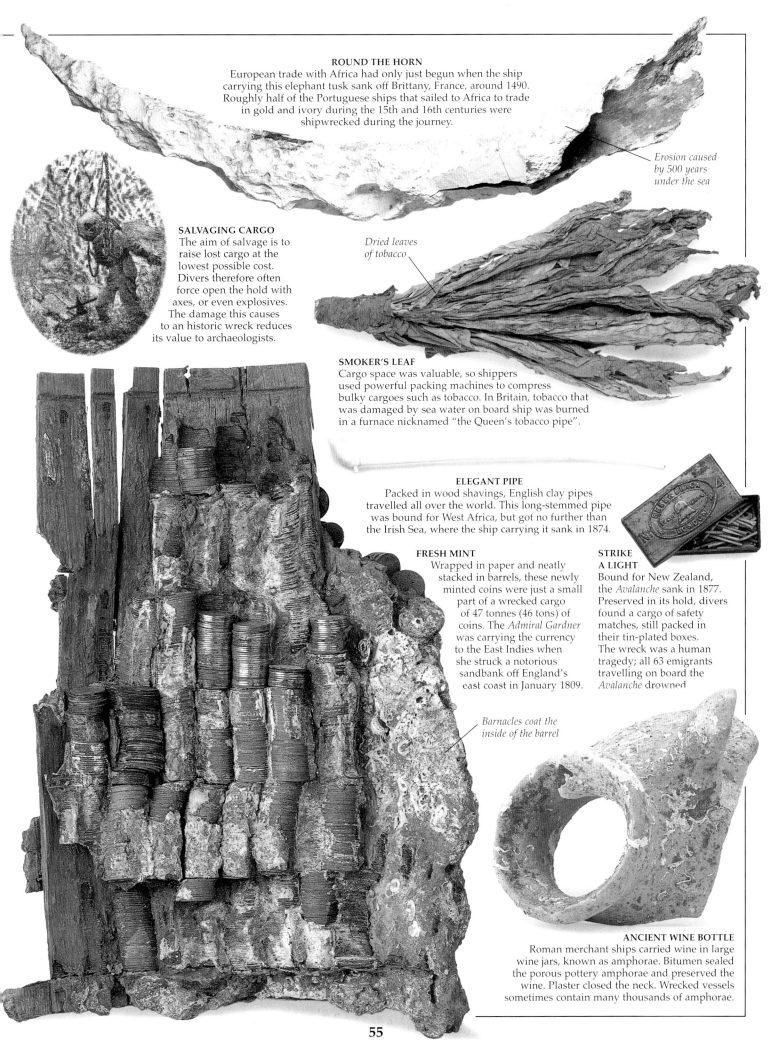

ROUND THE HORN
European trade with Africa had only just begun when the ship carrying this elephant tusk sank off Brittany, France, around 1490. Roughly half of the Portuguese ships that sailed to Africa to trade in gold and ivory during the 15th and 16th centuries were shipwrecked during the journey.

Erosion caused by 500 years under the sea

SALVAGING CARGO
The aim of salvage is to raise lost cargo at the lowest possible cost. Divers therefore often force open the hold with axes, or even explosives. The damage this causes to an historic wreck reduces its value to archaeologists.

Dried leaves of tobacco

SMOKER'S LEAF
Cargo space was valuable, so shippers used powerful packing machines to compress bulky cargoes such as tobacco. In Britain, tobacco that was damaged by sea water on board ship was burned in a furnace nicknamed "the Queen's tobacco pipe".

ELEGANT PIPE
Packed in wood shavings, English clay pipes travelled all over the world. This long-stemmed pipe was bound for West Africa, but got no further than the Irish Sea, where the ship carrying it sank in 1874.

FRESH MINT
Wrapped in paper and neatly stacked in barrels, these newly minted coins were just a small part of a wrecked cargo of 47 tonnes (46 tons) of coins. The *Admiral Gardner* was carrying the currency to the East Indies when she struck a notorious sandbank off England's east coast in January 1809.

STRIKE A LIGHT
Bound for New Zealand, the *Avalanche* sank in 1877. Preserved in its hold, divers found a cargo of safety matches, still packed in their tin-plated boxes. The wreck was a human tragedy; all 63 emigrants travelling on board the *Avalanche* drowned.

Barnacles coat the inside of the barrel

ANCIENT WINE BOTTLE
Roman merchant ships carried wine in large wine jars, known as amphorae. Bitumen sealed the porous pottery amphorae and preserved the wine. Plaster closed the neck. Wrecked vessels sometimes contain many thousands of amphorae.

Reconstruction and preservation

WHEN DIVERS HAVE FINISHED measuring and taking photographs of a wreck, they attempt to raise it from the ocean floor (pp. 50–51). Study and conservation begins on dry land. Objects made of hard materials such as stone may need only washing. Most, however, require further treatment. Timbers shrink, and iron objects like cannons sometimes corrode so quickly in air that they fizz and heat up. Museum conservators have developed treatments to stop or reverse this decay. Their most important task is to protect the finds for historians to study, but they also need to show them to the public. It is not always easy to do both. Objects that fascinate scholars may look like dull lumps of wood to museum visitors, and public display of a fragile treasure for one year can do more damage than a century spent under the sea.

CORAL BOTTLE
The tiny skeletons of dead sea creatures can add to the beauty of wreck artefacts. However, cleaning may mean destroying the beautiful lace-like coral growing on this bottle.

MUSICAL MOUTHFUL
Rust spreading from submerged iron objects cements everything nearby into a concretion (shapeless lump). Conservators use chisels to chip off the worst deposits. Electrolysis – passing electricity through metal objects in a chemical bath – slows further corrosion and softens concretions, making them easier to remove.

Cleaned harmonica

Harmonicas in concretion

BARNACLE BOWL
Though its hard glaze protects porcelain against damage, marine creatures often make their homes on crockery in wrecked cargoes. Here their abandoned shells coat a bowl from the Nanking cargo recovered from the Dutch East Indiaman *Geldermalsen*, which sank in 1752.

CLEANING UP
Scraping barnacles off porcelain would scratch its glaze. Rather than risk this, conservators soak the crockery in a dilute acid solution. The acid dissolves some of the crust, and softens the remainder, so that it washes off without risk of damage.

MEASURING UP

The measurement and study of artefacts raised from a wreck helps to establish the ship's age and purpose. The shape and size of amphorae (ancient jars), for example, can indicate roughly where they came from. By comparing the maker's stamp with a list compiled from thousands of other examples, it is even possible to identify the workshop that made a newly discovered jar.

THE BIG CLEANUP

Compared to the condition of most wrecks, archaeologists raised the *Vasa* (pp. 26–27) in a relatively complete state, but they still faced an enormous task. Eleven scientists worked for five months just to clean the hull which was made from 14,000 pieces. In all, 25,000 objects were found in and around the wreck. Reconstruction of the ship took nearly 20 years.

PICK UP THE PIECES

Before archaeologists could re-create this beautiful jug they had to document exactly where each piece of pottery lay on the seabed. The distribution of the fragments may reveal vital clues as to whether the pot broke before or after the wreck – and thus, perhaps, how the ship sank.

Barnacles have been removed with diluted acid

Spraying the Mary Rose *will take 15–20 years*

LET US SPRAY

If wood saturated with sea water dries, it shrinks and twists. To prevent this, conservators treat the timbers with a waxy chemical called polyethylene glycol (PEG). Small objects can be soaked in baths, but the only way to treat a whole wreck is to spray it with PEG over a period of several years.

RE-ERECTED WRECK

Tides and currents on the seabed can quickly spread a ship's timbers over a wide area. So once the wood has been stabilized with PEG, conservators attempt to reassemble the pieces of the hull like a giant jigsaw puzzle.

PRESERVATION

Though the crockery now looks perfect, sea water that has penetrated the glaze could crystalize, cracking the plate. Conservators prevent this by soaking the porcelain in a dilute salt solution, and gradually reduce the salt concentration over a period of months.

The art of shipwrecks

SHIPWRECKS HAVE ALWAYS fascinated writers, painters, and dramatists, but the very first shipwreck yarns were myths. These traditional stories often featured gods and heroes. Through myths ancient people tried to explain and understand natural forces that governed their lives. In later ages, shipwreck stories enthralled people because they were a terrifying, yet common, experience. Ships were the fastest way to travel, and ocean voyages were more dangerous than today. It is not hard to see why shipwrecks still catch the imagination of modern storytellers. Sea voyages bring together people of different characters and backgrounds. The wreck is a dramatic climax. Survival on a raft or island brings out the best – and worst – in everybody, and a rescue always provides a happy ending.

NOAH'S ARK
In the *Bible* God tells Noah of his plan to flood the Earth to cleanse it of evil. Noah builds a ship, the *Ark*, to save his family and the world's wildlife. After 40 days and nights of heavy rain, the *Ark* finally runs aground on Mount Ararat, Turkey.

JONAH AND THE WHALE
A *Bible* book named after Jonah describes his ordeal on a storm-tossed ship in the Mediterranean. Fearing that they will be wrecked, the crew draws lots to see who should be blamed for the squall. When Jonah loses, they throw him overboard, and a "great fish", believed to have been a whale, swallows the unfortunate mariner.

ROBINSON CRUSOE
Shipwrecked on a desolate island, Robinson Crusoe suffers terrible hardships, ranging from loneliness to cannibal attacks. English author Daniel Defoe invented the shipwreck featured in his novel, but based Crusoe on Alexander Selkirk (1676–1721), a Scottish sailor who argued with the captain of his ship and asked to be put ashore on a Pacific island.

WHISKY GALORE
When the *Politician* ran aground between the Scottish islands of Eriskay and South Uist in 1941, local people were eager to help unload its cargo – cases of whisky. In *Whisky Galore* British novelist Compton MacKenzie (1883–1972) turned the consequences of the wreck into hilarious fiction in 1947. A film followed in 1948.

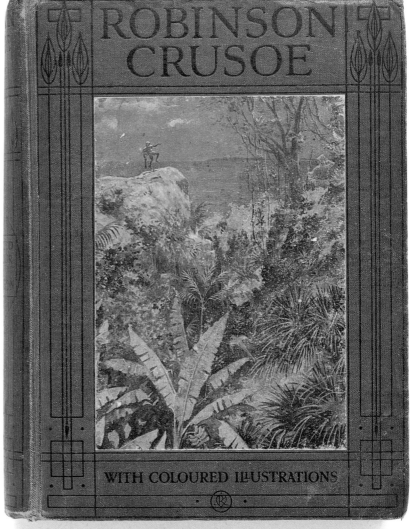

Robinson Crusoe novel

CUTTHROAT ISLAND
Sinking ships do not always make good films. In *Cutthroat Island* (1995) explosions destroy a pirate ship, but critics hated the film. They scorned the "dumb story line" and bad acting of the hero, played by Geena Davis, the Finnish-born director's wife

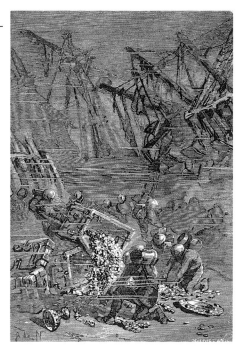

ULYSSES AND THE SIRENS
In his epic poem, the *Odyssey*, Greek writer Homer (800 BC) tells the myth of Ulysses, who narrowly escapes shipwreck when he sails past the island home of the Sirens. Half-woman, half-bird, these creatures lure passing mariners on to the rocky island with their sweet songs. Ulysses protects his crew by blocking their ears with wax. The crew then tie him to the mast – but leave his ears unblocked – so that he can enjoy the Sirens' calls.

20,000 LEAGUES UNDER THE SEA
French novelist Jules Verne (1828–1905) conjures up a fantastic underwater world of divers and submarines in his book *20,000 Leagues Under the Sea* (a league is 4 km or 2.15 miles), written in 1870. Verne's descriptions of diving equipment were incredibly accurate predictions of innovations to come.

SAINT NICHOLAS
According to Christian legends, Saint Nicholas saved the lives of his shipmates when storms threatened to wreck their little sailing boat off the coast of Turkey. This miracle made him the patron saint of sailors in danger. Also known as Santa Claus, Nicholas was in reality probably a 4th-century bishop of Myra, Turkey.

THE LITTLE MERMAID. 69

said she; "I know that I shall love the world up there, and all the people who live in it."

At last she reached her fifteenth year. "Well, now, you are grown up," said the old dowager, her grandmother; "so you must let me adorn you like your other sisters:" and she placed a wreath of white lilies in her hair, and every flower leaf was half a pearl. Then the old lady ordered eight great oysters to attach themselves to the tail of the princess to show her high rank.

"But they hurt me so!" said the little mermaid.

"Pride must suffer pain," replied the old lady. Oh, how gladly she would have shaken off all this grandeur, and laid aside the heavy wreath! The red flowers in her own garden would have suited her much better; but she could not help herself: so she said, "Farewell," and rose as lightly as a bubble to the surface of the water. The sun had just set as she raised her head above the waves; but the clouds were tinted with crimson and gold, and through the glimmering twilight beamed the evening star in all its beauty. The sea was calm, and the air mild and fresh. A large ship, with three masts, lay becalmed on the water, with only one sail set; for not a breeze stirred, and the sailors sat idle on deck or amongst the rigging. There was music and song on board; and, as darkness came on, a hundred coloured lanterns were lighted, as if the flags of all nations waved in the air. The little mermaid swam close to the cabin windows; and now and then, as the waves lifted her up, she could look in through clear glass window-panes, and see a number of well-dressed people within. Among them was a young prince, the most beautiful of all, with large black eyes; he was sixteen years of age, and his birthday was being kept with much rejoicing. The sailors were dancing on deck, but when the prince came out of the cabin, more than a hundred rockets rose in the air, making it as bright as day. The little mermaid was so startled that she dived under water: and when she again stretched out her head, it appeared as if all the stars of heaven were falling around her—she had never seen such fireworks before. Great suns spurted fire about, splendid fire-flies flew into the blue air, and everything was reflected in

"She rose as lightly as a bubble to the surface of the water."—p. 69.

THE CRUEL SEA
In the 1953 film *The Cruel Sea*, a small group of British sailors struggle to survive together on a raft after a submarine sinks their ship. The film's realistic view of plucky World War II (1939–1945) heroism made it hugely popular.

THE LITTLE MERMAID
When a terrifying storm wrecks a ship in this charming fairy story, the little mermaid of the title rescues a handsome prince from drowning beneath the ocean waves. To join him on land she swaps her beautiful voice for a pair of human legs. The story was one of 156 that Danish author Hans Christian Andersen (1805–1875) wrote.

Did you know?

AMAZING FACTS

The archaeological team working on the *Mary Rose* made an amazing 24,640 dives down to the wreck. If all the time the divers spent underwater is added together, it amounts to a total of 9 years spent on the seabed!

The wreck of the USS *Arizona*, which was sunk during the Japanese attack on Pearl Harbor in 1941, can still be seen in the sea off the island of Oahu, in Hawaii. The wreck was dedicated as a war memorial in 1962. Today visitors view the wreck from the Arizona Memorial building, which lies above it.

The Pharos lighthouse was one of the Seven Wonders of the Ancient World. It was built about 280 BC to warn ships of dangerous underwater rocks around the port of Alexandria in Egypt. The Pharos stood for nearly 1,500 years, until it was finally destroyed in an earthquake.

Archaeologists working on the wreck of the Kyrenia ship discovered the remains of almost 10,000 almonds. These freshly harvested nuts were part of the ship's cargo and could be dated to around 288 BC – giving a date for the sinking of the ship.

Almonds

Some wooden wrecks are badly damaged by a wood-devouring worm called the teredo. The larva of this worm bores into the wood, leaving only a tiny pinhole to show where it got in. Once inside, the teredo follows the grain of the wood, boring a tube about 8 mm (0.3 in) in diameter. Scientists calculated that, in the right conditions, teredo worms could completely devour most wooden shipwrecks within about 25 to 50 years!

Teredo worm

For many years, engineers in the Netherlands have been building dykes to reclaim land from the sea. When they drained an area called the Zuider Zee, the wrecks of over 350 ships were uncovered. The earliest ships date from the medieval period, but some sank in the more recent past.

Morse code messages, especially "SOS" calls, have saved thousands of sea travellers. The code was invented in 1838 by American, Samuel F. B. Morse. He sent the first message himself in 1844. It read, "What hath God wrought!"

The *Mary Rose* being raised from the seabed by a crane on board a barge

In 1836, two British divers, John and Charles Deane, first discovered the site of the wreck of the *Mary Rose*, off the southern coast of England. They tried to excavate the wreck using explosives, but luckily there was so much silt from the seabed lying on top of the ship that they did very little damage. The intact hull of the *Mary Rose* remained undisturbed for another 135 years.

In 1629, the *Batavia* was wrecked off the western coast of Australia. Most of the passengers and crew survived the wreck and came ashore on a nearby island. The captain and senior officers left in search of help and returned about 100 days later. They were horrified to discover that while they were away some of the survivors had mutinied and had senselessly massacred 125 of the others. As a result of both the massacre and the executions that followed it, only 68 of the original 316 people on board the ship survived.

In 1981, a property developer in New York City, USA, got quite a surprise when he discovered the remains of a sailing ship underneath a car park in Lower Manhattan. In the 18th century, the car park area had formed part of the city's harbour, although the water was quite shallow. As ships became bigger, this part of the harbour became too shallow and was soon unusable. It was then filled in with logs, stones, and soil to create new land. Old, unused ships, like the one discovered in 1981, were sometimes buried as landfill.

Quadrants, sextants, and octants were all navigation instruments used to calculate latitude – how far north or south a ship was positioned. Their names came from their shapes: a quadrant had a graduated arc of 90°, or a quarter of a circle; a sextant had an arc of 60°, or a sixth of a circle; and an octant had an arc of 45°, or an eighth of a circle.

Many battles have taken place on the lakes bordering the United States and Canada. In 1758, British troops at the southern end of Lake George sank hundreds of their own small boats so that the winter cold and ice would preserve them. Many sank too deep and are only now being raised.

In July 1281, almost 4,000 ships sank in one night. The ships were chained together as part of an attack on Japan instigated by the Mongol warrior leader Kublai Khan. It was a storm rather than retaliation that destroyed the ships, which were not found again until 1980.

A sextant in use

The *Titanic* leaves port on her fateful voyage.

Q Why did the *Titanic* sink?

A The *Titanic* collided with an iceberg in the North Atlantic Ocean. Survivors of the disaster said they had felt the iceberg scraping along the side of the ship, so experts assumed that it had ripped a long gash in the ship's hull. However, recent pictures from the *Titanic's* wreck site show no signs of this gash. Scientists now think that the impact of the collision buckled the seams between the plates of metal forming the hull. This caused them to separate from one another and allowed water to flood in and sink the ship.

Q How did early lighthouses make their light?

A Over the centuries, a variety of fuel sources have been used to provide the light in lighthouses. The Pharos had a "fire chamber" at the top, in which wood was burned in a series of huge torches. Later lighthouses used large candles made of tallow (melted-down animal fat) or burned peat or the more familiar fuels of coal, oil,

and gas. Electricity was finally introduced into lighthouses in the 1870s.

Q What happened to the crew of the *Mary Celeste*?

A In 1872, the *Mary Celeste* was found drifting in the Atlantic with no-one on board. She looked as if she had been abandoned in a great rush. There are several theories about what happened to the ten people on board. One theory is that they mutinied – the crew turned against the captain and deserted the ship. Another is that they fled because they thought that the cargo of alcohol was about to explode. No survivors were ever found, however, and no-one really knows what happened.

Q Why do some wrecks survive almost intact, while others rot away?

A It mainly depends where they sink. Marine worms

and other creatures that destroy wrecks cannot survive in water with low oxygen or salt levels, such as the Baltic Sea. This is why the hull of the *Vasa* was found in excellent condition after 328 years in the Baltic, whereas the woodwork on the *Titanic* had been destroyed after only 73 years in the Atlantic. Other factors, such as currents and temperature, also affect decay.

Record Breakers

⚓ THE GREATEST LOSS OF LIFE
On January 30, 1945, an estimated 8,000 people were killed when a soviet submarine torpedoed the German ship *Wilhelm Gustloff*. The ship was just off the coast of what is now Gdansk in Poland and was packed with civilian refugees, young female sailors, and wounded soldiers. Less than 1,000 survived.

⚓ WORLD'S TALLEST LIGHTHOUSE
Amazingly, the world's tallest lighthouse is still the first one ever built. The Pharos lighthouse at Alexandria, Egypt, was about 124 m (407 ft) tall. The structure was wider at the bottom than at the top to keep it stable.

Artist's interpretation of the Pharos lighthouse at Alexandria, Egypt

The "ghost ship" *Mary Celeste*

The Sinan ship was a junk, similar to this one.

Timeline

THERE HAVE BEEN SHIPWRECKS ever since people first started using boats. In many cases, there are no records of the ship, or the wreck had rotted away on the seabed and is forgotten. But many other wrecks are well documented, or are located in places where they are relatively easy to discover and so are found by fishermen or explorers. The timeline below lists just some of the ships that have been discovered over the past 3,000 years. There are probably many more wrecks still to be found.

• C. 1316 BC
THE ULUBURUN SHIP
A valuable cargo of gold, jewellery, glassware, and ingots of copper and tin is aboard the Uluburun ship that sinks off the coast of Turkey.

• C. 400 BC **THE KYRENIA SHIP**
A ship sinks off Kyrenia on the island of Cyprus in the Mediterranean Sea.

• AD 1323 **THE SINAN SHIP**
A Chinese junk carrying a cargo of porcelain from China to Japan is wrecked off the coast of Korea.

• 1545 **THE MARY ROSE**
During a naval display off southern England, the warship *Mary Rose* keels over and sinks. More than 650 crew members drown.

• 1588 **THE SPANISH ARMADA**
More than 30 ships from the Spanish Armada are wrecked on the coasts of the British Isles. About 11,000 sailors drown. Some ships are sunk in battle, but most are sunk by fierce storms off the coast of Ireland.

• 1628 **THE VASA**
The Swedish warship *Vasa* sets out across Stockholm harbour on her maiden voyage. She travels just 1,300 m (4,625 ft) before a gust of wind blows her over and sinks her, drowning at least 50 people.

• 1676 **THE WRECK OF THE KRONAN**
A squall on the Baltic is fatal for the enormous Swedish warship *Kronan*, which capsizes while turning around to fight a Danish–Dutch fleet.

Ivory statue from the *Mary Rose*

• 1690 **THE VUNG TAU JUNK**
A Chinese junk sinks off the port of Vung Tau, on the south coast of Vietnam. It is carrying a valuable cargo of porcelain made for export to the West.

• 1760 **THE RAMILLIES**
The English man-of-war, *Ramillies*, is shipwrecked in Bigbury Bay near Plymouth, UK. Hurricane-force winds drive the *Ramillies* on to the rocks and 700 people are drowned.

• 1813 **THE HAMILTON AND THE SCOURGE**
On Lake Ontario, between Canada and the USA, a fierce squall sinks two Great Lakes schooners, the *Hamilton* and the *Scourge*. Both ships had been recently converted to warships by the US to fight the British, but neither ship was suitable for the purpose.

• 1816 **THE MEDUSA**
The French ship *Medusa* runs aground off the coast of Africa. Some passengers and crew escape on a raft and drift at sea for 12 days. They survive by eating the flesh of their dead companions.

• 1820 **THE ESSEX**
The crew of the *Essex* escape in rowing boats after their ship is rammed by a whale in the Pacific Ocean. Some of the crew survive for 3 months by eating the bodies of those who have died. This incident inspires the novel *Moby Dick*.

• 1859 **THE ROYAL CHARTER**
While returning to the UK from Australia, the passenger and cargo ship *Royal Charter* is wrecked off the island of Anglesey in North Wales. In all, 459 people die.

• 1872 **THE MARIE CELESTE**
The sailing ship *Marie Celeste* is found drifting abandoned on the Atlantic Ocean. No-one has ever discovered what happened to her crew.

• 1882 **THE DUORO**
The British mail ship *Duoro* collides with a Spanish vessel and sinks in the Bay of Biscay, off Spain. Most of the passengers and crew escape, but the *Duoro's* cargo of diamonds, gold, and coffee is lost.

• 1900 **DISCOVERY OF THE ANTIKYTHERA SHIP**
A local sponge diver discovers the wreck of a Roman cargo ship off the Greek island of Antikythera. The wreck contains statues and other art treasures.

• 1906 **DISCOVERY OF THE RAMILLIES**
Divers discover the wreck of the *Ramillies* in Bigbury Bay, UK, and retrieve many artefacts.

The English take on the Spanish Armada in the 1588 Battle of Gravelines.

Banknotes recovered from the *Titanic*

• 1912 THE TITANIC
The luxury ocean liner *Titanic* is hit by an iceberg on her maiden voyage from the UK to the USA. She sinks in the North Atlantic, drowning more than 1,500 passengers and crew. It remains one of the worst ever peacetime shipping disasters.

• 1913 THE KARLUK
The Canadian exploration ship *Karluk* is trapped in the Arctic ice and crushed. Some of the crew survive for nearly a year on an Arctic island before they are rescued.

• 1915 THE LUSITANIA
During World War I, the British ocean liner *Lusitania* is torpedoed by a German U-boat in the Atlantic. She sinks and 1,198 people are drowned. The loss of the liner and so many passengers, some of whom were American, helps to persuade the USA to enter the war against the Germans.

USS *Arizona* sinking after the Japanese attack on Pearl Harbor

• 1941 PEARL HARBOR
A Japanese aerial attack on the US naval base at Pearl Harbor on Oahu Island, Hawaii, results in the sinking of five battleships – the *Arizona*, *Oklahoma*, *California*, *Nevada*, and *West Virginia*. The most horrific sinking is that of the *Arizona*, which eventually explodes and is then hit by approximately eight more bombs. The attack precipitates the entry of the USA into World War II.

• 1956 DISCOVERY OF THE VASA
Swedish naval historian Anders Franzen discovers the wreck of the *Vasa* in Stockholm harbour. She is raised in 1961 and is now on display in a museum in Stockholm.

• 1971 DISCOVERY OF THE MARY ROSE
Divers discover the wreck of the *Mary Rose* off southern England. She is later raised and is now being preserved in Portsmouth harbour.

• 1975 DISCOVERY OF THE HAMILTON AND THE SCOURGE
Scientists using side-scan sonar locate the wrecks of the *Scourge* and the *Hamilton* in Lake Ontario.

• 1984 DISCOVERY OF THE ULUBURUN WRECK
A sponge diver discovers the Uluburun wreck off the coast of Turkey.

Arizona's masts and superstructure were all that could be seen above the smoke.

• 1985 DISCOVERY OF THE TITANIC
Scientists from Woods Hole Oceanographic Institution in the USA discover the wreck of the *Titanic*, using a remote-controlled submersible. In 1987, a French team lifts hundreds of objects from the wreck using a submarine with mechanical arms.

• 1989 THE EXXON VALDEZ
The *Exxon Valdez* oil tanker runs aground on the coast of Alaska, USA. One-sixth of its cargo of oil escapes into the sea, and pollutes a stretch of coastline 2,000 km (1,250 miles) long.

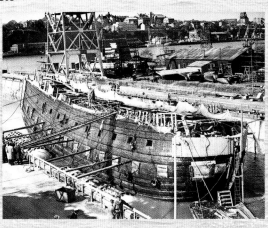

Recovery of the *Vasa*

• 1995 DISCOVERY OF THE DUORO
A salvage team locates the wreck of the *Duoro* in the Bay of Biscay.

• 2000 EXPLOSION ON THE KURSK
On August 12, an explosion on board a Russian nuclear-powered submarine sinks the vessel and tragically kills all 118 crew.

Find out more

Coins recovered from the *Mary Rose*

ONE OF THE MOST EXCITING things about shipwrecks is that they are still being discovered. Fascinating treasures from unknown ancient sailing ships and relatively modern ships, such as the *Titanic*, are still being recovered. Websites, such as those suggested on page 65, and information from libraries and bookstores will help you keep up to date with the latest discoveries. One of the best ways to bring the past to life is to actually see it for yourself. Use the information here to help you locate places where you can see real artefacts up close.

VISIT A LIFEBOAT STATION
At some lifeboat stations, you can see the lifeboats and find out about how they are launched, what equipment they carry, and some of the rescues they have been involved in. You can locate lifeboat stations in the UK and the Republic of Ireland that you can visit by looking at the RNLI website (p. 65).

SEE A RAISED WRECK
Some shipwrecks have been raised from the sea. Information about visiting the *Mary Rose* and the *Vasa* is given on page 65, but there are other shipwrecks you can visit. For example, you can see the wreck of the pirate ship *Whydah* and many exciting artefacts found near it at an exhibition centre in Provincetown, Massachusetts, USA.

The 17th-century warship *Vasa* on display in Stockholm

VISIT A MUSEUM
Many maritime museums have fascinating exhibits and information about shipwrecks. In the UK, you could visit Greenwich Maritime Museum in London, but there are many more around the world, such as the National Maritime Museum in Sydney, Australia.

Places to Visit

THE MARY ROSE, PORTSMOUTH, UK
The *Mary Rose* is the only 16th-century warship on display in the world. The wreck was recovered in 1982 and is in the process of being preserved. Thousands of 16th-century objects from the wreck are displayed nearby.

THE CHARLESTOWN SHIPWRECK CENTRE, ST. AUSTELL, CORNWALL, UK
A collection of artefacts and treasure rescued from shipwrecks, including articles from the wreck of the *Ramillies* (p. 20).

NATIONAL MARITIME MUSEUM, GREENWICH, LONDON, UK
This is the world's largest maritime museum. It contains around two million items, from real boats and heavy machinery to naval costumes and navigation instruments.

THE VASA MUSEUM, STOCKHOLM, SWEDEN
This is Scandinavia's most-visited museum. It centres around the restored warship *Vasa* – the only remaining intact 17th-century ship in the world. Star exhibits include the restored hull of the *Vasa*, permanent exhibitions about the ship's lifting and restoration, and a lightship and an icebreaker.

SOUTH STREET SEAPORT MUSEUM, NEW YORK CITY, USA
Located at the site of city's historic port, exhibits and events at this museum connect the USA's maritime history with its impact on the present.

AUSTRALIAN NATIONAL MARITIME MUSEUM, SYDNEY, AUSTRALIA
A huge museum dedicated to ships and Australia's maritime history.

MORSE CODE

A •—	N —•
B —•••	O ———
C —•—•	P •——•
D —••	Q ——•—
E •	R •—•
F ••—•	S •••
G ——•	T —
H ••••	U ••—
I ••	V •••—
J •———	W •——
K —•—	X —••—
L •—••	Y —•——
M ——	Z ——••

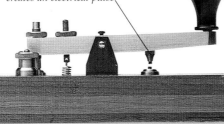

When this piece of metal contacts the bit below, it creates an electrical pulse

Morse code machine

SEND A MORSE CODE MESSAGE
Have fun with your friends by learning Morse code and using it to send secret messages. The key to the code is shown above. Remember, you could send a Morse message as sound, flashes of light on a torch, or even written down. If you are in a hurry to code a long message, go to the Morse code website given in the *Useful Websites* box. It will do an instantaneous translation for you.

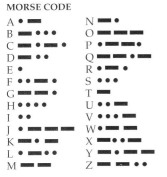

The railings at the ship's bow

Figurehead of Queen Victoria in Los Angeles Maritime Museum, California, USA

USEFUL WEBSITES

- The website for the *Mary Rose*
  www.maryrose.org
- The *Vasa* Museum's website
  www.vasamuseet.se/indexeng.html
- The website for the RNLI (Royal National Lifeboat Institution)
  www.rnli.org.uk/Home.asp
- The National Maritime Museum, London, UK
  www.nmm.ac.uk
- The Charlestown Shipwreck Centre, St. Austell, UK
  www.shipwreckcharlestown.com
- These *Titanic* websites display pictures of real artefacts; the second one gives dates and places for the touring exhibition.
  www.discovery.com/stories/science/sciencetitanic/sciencetitanic.html
  www.titanic-online.com/titanic/index.html
- This website has a morse code translator
  www.scouting.org/fun/morse/index.html
- Links to maritime museums and shipwreck websites
  www.anthro.org/marine2.htm
- An enormous database of shipwreck websites
  www.mysteries-megasite.com/main/bigsearch/shipwreck-1.html

THE TITANIC
Probably the most famous shipwreck in the world is that of the *Titanic*. The sinking of the so-called "unsinkable" ship in 1912 has inspired many books and a blockbuster film. Various expeditions have visited the wreck site, bringing back photographs, film footage, and artefacts. You can see many of these on the internet (two websites are given in the box on the right), and there is also a touring exhibition of artefacts, which you may be able to visit. Dates and places for the exhibition are given on the second website.

Glossary

AIR-SEA RESCUE Rescuing people from the sea using a helicopter.

AMPHORA A type of large jar used by the Ancient Greeks and Romans. An amphora had a narrow neck and two handles, and was often used for transporting oil or wine.

AQUALUNG A type of breathing equipment used by divers. It consists of a cylinder of compressed air strapped to the diver's back, and connected by a tube to a mouthpiece, which automatically feeds air to the diver.

ARCHAEOLOGIST A person who studies human history by excavating ancient or historic sites and analyzing the buildings and remains found there. A marine archaeologist is someone who examines the wrecks of ships.

ARTEFACT A human-made object. Archaeologists investigate artefacts found on shipwrecks to learn more about the lives and skills of the people who once owned them.

ASTROLABE A navigation instrument used to check a ship's route by measuring the position of the Sun.

BACKSTAFF A navigation instrument. Like an astrolabe, the backstaff established the ship's latitude by measuring the position of the Sun.

BALLAST Any heavy material placed in a ship to make it more stable.

BARNACLES Small sea creatures with hard shells. Barnacles often cling to rocks, ship's bottoms, or objects from a shipwreck.

BILGE The lowest part of a ship's hull. Dirty water, called "bilge water", often collects in the bilges.

BOW The front of a ship.

Amphora

BRIDGE The part of a ship that houses the wheel and the navigation instruments, and from where the captain and other officers direct operations.

BUOY A floating marker anchored to the seabed by a chain or cable. A buoy indicates the position of a hazard to ships, such as rocks or a reef.

CAPSIZE To overturn a boat.

CARGO Goods carried on board a ship.

CHRONOMETER An instrument for measuring time, similar to a clock, used to help navigate at sea. A chronometer keeps the correct time even if it is shaken about or subjected to changing temperatures or humidity.

CONCRETION A hard, sold mass. For example, when iron objects are submerged in seawater for a long time they produce rust, which sticks everything nearby into a hard lump, or concretion.

DIVING BELL An open-bottomed bell or box with an air supply, in which a diver can descend into deep water.

FIGUREHEAD A carving, such as a bust or a full-length figure, attached to the prow of a ship. The figurehead was supposed to bring good luck.

FIRE SHIP A ship deliberately set on fire in the hope that it will either burn enemy ships or cause them to retreat in fear of catching alight.

FLEET A group of battleships operating together under one command.

FOGHORN A loud horn sounded from the coast or from a ship during foggy weather to warn other ships that there is danger ahead.

GALLEON A Spanish warship.

GPS A modern navigation aid that uses signals from a series of satellites circling the Earth to establish a ship's position. GPS is short for Global Positioning Satellites.

GUN CARRIAGE A large wooden block on wheels that is used to support a cannon or other large gun.

GUNPORT Openings in the side of a ship through which cannons and other heavy guns were fired. In many cases, they could be closed in bad weather.

Figurehead

HELMSMAN The person who steers a ship.

HULL The main body of a ship.

HURRICANE A gigantic revolving tropical storm. A hurricane can also be called a cyclone or a typhoon.

Junk

JUNK A chinese sailing ship with a flat-bottomed hull and lifting rudder.

KEEL A ship's lowest longitudinal, or lengthwise, timbers, on which the hull is built. The word can also mean to capsize.

LATITUDE A system for expressing a ship's position. It shows how far north or south of the equator a ship is. It is often expressed in degrees and minutes, for example, 10° 20' N.

LIFEBOAT A small boat carried on a larger ship for use in an emergency. For example, if the ship was sinking, the passengers and crew could escape in a lifeboat. A lifeboat can also be a boat launched from the land to rescue people who are in danger at sea.

LIGHTSHIP A ship that is moored or anchored in one position and carries a beacon light to warn other ships of a potential danger, such as hidden rocks.

A diver using scuba equipment

LONGITUDE A system for expressing a ship's position. It shows how far a ship is to the east or west of a designated line, called the prime meridian. It is often expressed in degrees and minutes, for example, 20° 15' W.

MAIDEN VOYAGE A ship's first voyage.

MAN-OF-WAR Another name for a warship or battleship. It is mostly used to describe the large, old sailing ships once used for battle.

MARINE Used to describe things that are in the sea or that relate to the sea in some way.

MAYDAY An international radio distress signal used to summon help by ships that are in danger. The word is based on the French expression *m'aidez*, which means "help me".

MERCHANT VESSEL A ship used to transport goods, rather than a warship.

MESS A place on board a ship where a group of people eat their meals. For example, the "officers' mess" is the place where the ship's captain and other officers eat their meals.

METEOROLOGIST A scientist who studies and forecasts the weather.

MORSE CODE A code in which the letters of the alphabet are represented by combinations of long and short pulses of light or sound. Morse code was invented in 1838 by Samuel Morse and was often used at sea.

NAVAL VESSEL A warship that forms part of a country's navy.

NAVIGATE To direct the course of a ship.

PORT The left-hand side of a ship.

POSH This word now means smart or elegant but it used to be an acronym for "Port Over, Starboard Home". This was once the location of the desired shady cabins on a journey from England to Asia and back.

ROV An underwater vehicle that is operated remotely from a ship and does not carry a crew. ROVs are used to film or photograph wrecks that sunk in very deep water, and sometimes to bring back objects from the seabed. ROV stands for Remotely Operated underwater Vehicle.

SALVAGE The retrieval of cargo or other objects from a wreck.

SCUBA Another name for an aqualung. Scuba is an acronym for Self-Contained Underwater Breathing Apparatus.

SEMAPHORE A signalling system that uses two coloured flags in various positions to indicate the letters of the alphabet.

SEXTANT A navigation instrument that enabled a navigator to establish the position of the Sun relative to the horizon, and from this, work out the ship's latitude.

SHIPWRIGHT A person who builds ships.

SIDE-SCAN SONAR A form of sonar used to survey large areas of the seabed. It uses sound waves to produce a "shadow" photograph of any features or objects on the bottom of the ocean.

SNORKEL A short breathing tube used by divers who are swimming just below the surface of the water. One end of the tube sticks up above the surface of the water, while the diver holds the other end in his or her mouth.

SONAR A system used to locate objects on the seabed by sending out pulses of sound. The echoes of these sounds can be turned into a picture on a computer. Sonar is short for SOund Navigation And Ranging.

SOS A Morse-code signal sent out by ships in danger to appeal for help. The letters "SOS" do not stand for anything – they were chosen because they are easy to send and do not often occur together in a normal message.

STARBOARD The right-hand side of a ship.

STERN The back end of a ship.

Sextant

STERN-POST RUDDER A rudder that is in line with the ship's keel.

SUBMARINE An underwater vessel that carries crew and can stay under the sea for long periods of time.

SUBMERSIBLE An underwater vessel that stays under water only for short periods.

WATER-LINE The line along which the surface of the water touches a ship's side.

WET SUIT A tight-fitting rubber suit worn by divers to keep themselves warm in cold water and to protect their skin. A wet suit allows a thin layer of the water inside the fabric. This layer warms up with the diver's body heat and then helps to insulate the diver from the cold water all around.

Submarine

Eyewitness titles in this series:

Ancient Egypt	Pyramid
Ancient Greece	Religion
Ancient Rome	Rock & Mineral
Bird	Shark
Castle	Skeleton
Crystal & Gem	Space Exploration
Future	Viking
Medieval Life	Volcano
Music	Weather
Pirate	

Whale

Horse

Insect

Knight

Mammal

Mummy

Plant

Pond & River

Seashore

Shakespeare

Shipwreck

Victorians

Future titles to include:

Arms & Armour

Dance

Dinosaur

Early People

Explorer

Flying Machine

Fossil

Invention

Jungle

Ocean

Index

A

air hose 45
airlift 50
air-sea rescue 9, 41, 66
Aldis lamp 37
amphorae 50, 55, 57, 66
anchor and chain 42
Anderson, Hans Christian 59
Andrea Doria 9
Antikythera ship 15, 62
aqualung 46, 66
archaeologist 60, 66
Arctic 11, 38
Argo 28
Arles IV 50
Arun class lifeboat 41
astrolabe 22, 32, 33, 66
Atlantic Ocean 28, 61
atmospheric diving suit 48

B

backstaff 32, 66
ballast 17, 66
Baltic Sea 61, 62, 63
banknotes 54, 63
barnacles 56, 66
baryocyclometer 11
Bass, George 13, 49
Batavia 60
beach hose 31
beacon 34, 36
beak 27
bell, ship's 37
Bible 58
Bigbury Bay 20, 62, 63
bilge 42, 66
birds, oiled 31
Biscay, Bay of 21, 62
boathook 42
books 13, 58, 59, 64
boom 30
Borelli, Giovanni 44
Braer 30
breathing apparatus 45, 46
bridge 33, 42, 66
British Navy 18, 20, 24
Bullimore, Tony 39
buoyancy control device 46
buoys 10, 11, 35, 66

C

camera, head-mounted 9
Canaanite ship 13
cannon 14, 18, 24
Carew, Sir George 18, 19
cargoes 54, 55, 60, 62, 66
carronade 25
Chappé, Claude 37
chart plotter 42
charts and maps 32
Chinese ships 16, 17, 33, 62, 63
Chipchase liferaft 38
chronometer 33, 66
closed-circuit diving apparatus 45
coastline 31, 32, 42
Coffin, Owen 38
coins 8, 54, 55, 64
collapsible lifeboat 39
Colomb, Admiral Philip 37
communications 36, 37, 44
compass 32, 33
computer 42, 50, 65
concretion 29, 56, 66
conservation 56, 57
Cooper, James Fenimore 25
coral 10, 47, 56
Cousteau, Jacques 46
Crescent City 8
The Cruel Sea 59
cutlery 20, 26, 53

D E F

Darling, Grace 34
Davis, John 32
Deane, John and Charles 14, 60
deck-seat lifeboat 38
decompression chamber 48
deep-sea exploration 48, 49
Defoe, Daniel 58
demand valve 45, 46
distress calls 36
distress rocket 37
divers 9, 13, 44–47, 60, 67
diving bell 14, 44, 66
diving suit 14, 45, 47, 48, 49
drink 20, 52
drogue 43
Duoro 21, 62, 63
echo-sounder 42
Eddystone lighthouse 35
electrolysis 56
English Channel 10
Essex 38, 62
Exxon Valdez 30, 31, 63

figurehead 24, 29, 65, 66
films 59, 65
fire-fighting equipment 42
fires 30, 42
fire ship 22, 66
flags 36
flares 37, 42
fog 10
foghorn 34, 36, 66
forecastle 19
Franzén, Anders 27, 63

G H I

Gagnan, Emile 46
George, Lake 60
Géricault, Théodore 38
German lifeboat 41
ghost ship 9, 61
Girona 22, 23
GPS (global positioning satellite) 33, 66
Gravelines, Battle of 22
Greathead lifeboat 40
Greeks 8, 12, 15, 32, 44
gun carriage 27, 52, 66
gunpowder measure 52
Hamilton 24, 25, 62, 63
harmonica 53
Harrison, John 33
helicopter 9, 35, 41, 43
helmet, diving 44, 45
Henry VIII 18
Hillary, William 40
Homer 59
hurricane 11, 62, 66
iceberg 28, 61
inflatable lifeboat 41; liferaft 39

J K L

Japan 60, 62
Jet fins 47
Jonah and the whale 58
junks 16, 17, 66
Karluk 38, 63
knife, dive 47
Kronan 62
Kursk 63
Kyrenia ship 12, 60, 62
lading 54
lamps 35, 37
latitude 32, 66
Lethbridge, John 44
Lichfield 10
life on ship 19, 20, 21, 26, 52, 53
lifeboat, rescue 8, 40, 64;

equipment 42, 43
lifeboat, ship's 29, 38, 39, 66
life buoy 43
life jacket 43
liferaft 38, 39, 62
lighthouse 34, 35, 61
lightship 34, 65, 66
Little Mermaid, The 59
locating wrecks 50, 51
longitude 32, 33, 67
Lusitania 63

M

MacKenzie, Compton 58
magnetometer 50
mail ship 21
mapping wrecks 50, 51
marine life 9, 20, 56
Mary Celeste 9, 61, 62
Mary Rose 14, 18, 19, 57, 60, 62, 64, 65
mask, diving 45, 46
matches 55
Mediterranean Sea 12, 13, 58, 62
Medusa 38, 62
Melville, Herman 38
mess 53, 67
Moby Dick 38, 62
Morse code 36, 37, 60, 65, 67
music 53, 59
Myers, Ned 25
myths 58

N O P

Nautile submarine 29, 67
navigation 9, 22, 32, 33, 42, 67
navigational buoy 35
Newt suit 49
Noah's ark 58
Nore lightship 34
ocean liner 28, 29
octant 60
Odyssey 59
oil tanker 30, 31
Ontario, Lake 24, 25, 62
Owen, Samuel 8
pack ice 11, 38
paintings 8, 38
Pandora 11
Pearl Harbor 60, 63
Peress, Joseph 48
pharmacy 52
Pharos lighthouse 34, 60, 61
Philip II 22
Phillips, Jack 29

pile lighthouse 35
pirates 17, 22, 64
pistol 53
pollution 30, 31
Polo, Marco 16
polyethylene glycol 57
porcelain 16, 17, 56, 57
Poseidon statue 15

Q R

quadrant 60
radar 9, 33, 34
radio 29, 37, 42
radio beacons 33, 39
raising wrecks 50, 51
Ramillies 20, 52, 62, 65
reconstruction 56, 57
reindeer hides 54
RNLI 40, 64, 65
Robinson Crusoe 58
Roman ships 15, 34, 62
rope and pulley 42, 43
ROV (remotely operated underwater vehicle) 25, 67
Royal Charter 21, 62
Royal George 14
rudder, stern-post 16, 17, 67

rust 29, 56, 66

S

sailing ships 9
Saint Nicholas 59
salvage 14, 54, 55, 67
sandbank 10
scissors 53
Scourge 24, 25, 62, 63
scuba diving 9, 46, 47, 67
scuttles 21
Sea Empress 30
self-righting lifeboat 40
Selkirk, Alexander 58
semaphore 36, 37, 67
sextant 32, 60, 67
Shetlands 30
side-scan sonar 25, 50, 67
Siebe, Augustus 45
signalling lamp 37
silt removal 50
Sinan ship 16, 62
Sirens 59
skeletons 26
snorkel 46, 67
Solent 18
sonar 25, 34, 50, 51, 67
SOS 29, 36, 60, 67
sounding weight 53

Spain 15
Spanish Armada 22, 23, 33, 62
speedline device 42
steam clipper 21
Stefansson, Vilhjalmur 38
storms 9, 52
stretcher 8, 43
submarine 29, 67, 63
submersibles 28, 29, 49, 67
sundial 32
surveys 50, 51
survivors 38, 39
Swedish Navy 26, 62
swimming 10

T U V

telescope 36
thirst 38
Titanic 28, 29, 37, 39, 61, 63, 65
tobacco 55
toothbrush 3
torch, underwater 47
treasure 8, 13, 15, 21
Turkish lifeboat 41
20,000 Leagues under the

Sea 59
U-boat 63
Uluburun ship 12, 13, 62, 63
Ulysses 59
United States Navy 24
Vasa 14, 26, 27, 57, 62, 63, 64, 65
Verne, Jules 59
Very, Edward 37
Vung Tau junk 16, 17, 62

W

warships 14, 18, 20, 22, 27, 62, 63
waves 10
weather buoy 11
weights, dive 45, 46, 47
wet suit 47, 67
whales 38, 58, 62
Whisky Galore 58
Whydah 64
wigwag code 36
Wilhelm Gustloff 61
winch 43
wind 9, 10, 11
wireless telegraphy 37
worms, marine 60, 61
wreck buoy 10

Acknowledgements

Dorling Kindersley would like to thank:
Derek King, Georgette Purches, and Gill Mace of the RNLI for their invaluable assistance; Charlestown Shipwreck and Heritage Centre, Richard and Bridget Larn; Ocean Leisure, London; Martin Dean and Steve Liscoe at the Archaeological Diving Unit, St. Andrews; Jim Pulack at the Institute of Nautical Archaeology, Texas, USA; the Vasa Museum, Stockholm; Simon Stevens, Gloria Clifton, and Barbara Tomlinson of the National Maritime Museum, London; Alan Hills at the British Museum; and Darren Trougton, Diane Clouting, Julie Ferris, Carey Scott, Nicki Waine, and Nicola Studdart for their editorial and design assistance.
Endpapers: Anna Martin
Index: Chris Bernstein

Picture credits
The publisher would like to thank the following for their kind permission to reproduce their photographs.
t=top, b=below, c=centre, l=left, r=right

Archaeological Diving Unit, St. Andrew's University 9br; **Bridgeman Art Library** 8cl, 11tr, 15tl, 15cr, 22tr, 22cl, 58tr, 59tl; **Jean Loup Charmet** 34c; **Christie's Images** 16br, 17tl, 17b; **Bruce Coleman** 9tr, 10tr; **Mary Evans Picture Library** 9bl, 14cl, 16tl, 20bl, 28tl, 29tc, 32cl, 36tr, 37tl, 38tl, 59tr; **E.T. Archive** 17tr, 17cr; **Sonia Halliday** 58cl, 59cl; **Robert Harding Picture Library** 10c; **Hulton-Getty** 24tr, 37bc, 44cl; **Ronald Grant Archive** 58bl; **Susan and Michael Katzev/I.N.A.** 12bl, 12c; **Image Select** 45bl; **I.N.A.** (Institute of Nautical Archaeology), Texas, USA 13tl, 13tr, 13cl, 13cr, 13bl, 13br/

National Geographic/Mr Bates Littlehales 49tl, 50br; **Kobal Collection** 59bl; **Mary Rose Preservation Trust** 18c, 18b, 19tr, 19c, 57br; **Mansell Collection** 44cr, 55tl; **Nantucket Historical Association** 38c; **National Geographic Image Collection**/Edward Kim 16bl, 16c, 16cr/Emory Kristof 24bl, 24–25bc/Richard Schlecht 25tr/Hamilton Scourge Foundation 25br; **National Maritime Museum, London** 14c, 15tr, 21tl, 21br, 22–23b, 60br, 62tl, 65br, 66bl, 66cr/**R.M.S. Titanic, Inc.** 28–29b, 32c, 32b, 33tl, 33tc, 33c, 36bc, 53tc; Bjorn Landstorm/Vasa Museum 26tr; **Pepys Library**, Magdelene College, Cambridge 18tr; **Planet Earth Pictures** 46cl; **Popperphoto** 9tl; Portsmouth City Council Museums and Record Service 14bl; R.A.F. Culdrose 35cl; **Rex Features** 9tc, 10bl, 19tl, 33tr, 39cr, 43bc, 47tr, 52c, 56cr, 59tc; **RNLI** 34cl, 40c, 41tr, 41c, 41cr, 42tl;

Alexis Rosenfeld 48–49b, 49tr, 49br, 50bl, 50tr, 50trc, 50c, 57tl; **Science Museum**, London, 67tr; **Science Photo Library** 11bl/Klein Associates 25tl, 30tr, 30bl, 31tl, 31tr, 31bc; **Frank Spooner** 30–31c/Gamma 31cr, 31br, 49cr; **Sygma** 29tl, 29tr, 29ct, 29c, 29cr, 30cl; **Telegraph Colour Library** 33br, 41tl, 50–51; **Ulster Museum**, Belfast 22c, 22bl, 23tl, 23tc, 23tr; **Vasa Museum**, Stockholm 26c, 26cl, 26bl, 26–27b, 27tl, 27tr, 27c, 27br, 57c; **Weidenfeld and Nicolson Archives** 38bl; **Zefa** 10cl, 10cr, 33cr, 35c.

Every effort has been made to trace the copyright holders. Dorling Kindersley apologizes in advance for any unintentional omissions, and would be pleased, in such cases, to add an acknowledgement in any subsequent editions.